W9-CFH-459

THE CROWD,
THE CRITIC,
AND THE MUSE

THE CROWD, THE CRITIC, AND THE MUSE:

A BOOK FOR CREATORS

güngör

WOODSLEY PRESS

©2012 Michael Gungor

All rights reserved. No portion of this book may be reproduced, stored in a retrieval system, or transmitted in any form or by any means—electronic, mechanical, photocopy, recording, scanning, or other—except for brief quotations in critical reviews or articles, without prior written permission of the author.

Book Design by Kristeen Ott
Editing by Patton Dodd
Illustrations by Josh Harvey

ISBN -
LCCN -

Published in Denver, Colorado by Woodsley Press.

In some instances, names, dates, locations and other details have been purposefully changed to protect the identities and privacy of those discussed in this book.

Printed in the United States of America

Woodsley
Press

For Lisa

INTRODUCTION : BREATH

Burnout is what happens when you try to avoid being human for too long.

It's awful—like the blood has been drained from your body, the breath emptied from your lungs. Still, the world is obstinate in its demands.

Produce!

Perform!

You just . . . can't . . . get air, but they keep telling you to sing, and they expect it to be in tune.

My wife and I were sitting in a minivan in a parking lot when I realized I had burned out. I saw it in her face, in her tears. These were not the good kind of tears. Not the palatable "she's just being emotional" or even the "she must be really pissed" kind. No, these were the ones that leak from a wound. The shy tears that spill from averted gazes and lowered heads. The worst kind.

I had hurt her, but I hadn't realized that I was doing it. I was too disconnected. Jaded. Fading. As the love of my life wiped the tears from her eyes and looked back into mine, I knew the pain in those eyes was my doing. And in that pain, I saw the shadow of the decrepit, feeble ghost that had once been my soul.

In the minivan, I realized that it wasn't external circumstances that were responsible for my numb detachment from the world. It wasn't the economy or the music industry that was to blame for the formless void that filled what used to be a passion for my work. It was the groundlessness of my internal world. This was the reason I hadn't written anything for months. Only real things get to create things, not ghosts or phantoms.

Dead souls do not produce the same stuff as living ones do.

Also, it wasn't organized religion that was responsible for me not knowing how to believe in anything anymore. It was because the mechanism that believes had been silenced.

Those tears were some of the collateral damage of a quieted soul.

I realized that something in me needed to change, and it needed to change quickly. I needed to get my feet on solid ground. So I did what you would expect any twenty-nine-year-old male to do—I surfed the Internet. That night when I got home, I Googled "best spiritual retreats in the world." (Yes, I trust John Google implicitly. And yes, sometimes I personify technology.)

The retreat that spawned from the tears in the minivan changed my life, but I'll tell you more about that later. For now, what matters is that the decision to tend the ground that I was living and creating from was the most important decision that I could have made. Actually, I was surprised to discover that as soon as I decided to go ahead with my retreat, something immediately began to soften and shift in me. The decision to take care of my soul was like stepping into a river. I could feel it pulling me towards something like a waterfall, like life itself was pulling me to its source.

Sometimes you have to take a step back in order to see the beauty of something. From the ledge of the Grand Canyon, Beauty shines bright as the sun. She wears a dress of granite and sky with sparkling shoes made of rushing river. Her eyes shine with sunbeams shading cliffs and valleys with color and shadow, revealing scope and texture. Her hair smells like wildflowers in the crisp desert wind. It's difficult to stand on the ledge of the Grand Canyon and not notice her presence.

But if you hike to the bottom of the Grand Canyon and lay prostrate with your face against the rocky floor, your awareness of her will soon begin to wane. All you see down there is rock. Maybe some dirt or a crawling bug.

These are the threads of her dress, but so close to the details, it's easy to lose sight of her essence.

This is a book for creators—for those down in the valley with the dirt and the bugs. That is where the real work of creation happens, not up in ivory towers or scenic overlooks, but with blistered hands and stained clothes. Still, in the dirt it is easy to lose perspective over time. Easy to see rock rather than canyon, thread rather than dress—easy to be so focused on the single word in the lyric that you can lose sight of the song or of why you make music in the first place.

Most of us don't have the luxury of living on the ledge of the canyon— there is too much work to be done. Still, the occasional day trip up to the overlook can serve us well. The productive artist knows that there is too much work to do to sit around and philosophize about art all day, but she also knows that the work of the details stems from the vision of the whole.

Art begins deep in the psyche. Down where the ideas like "self," "meaning," and "God" stew. Artists are not driven just by a vision for a specific work of art. They are driven by their vision of work itself—and of what it means to be human.

This is a book for creators who might need a reminder of why they do what they do. It is for those in need of breath. It is a trail guide to the edge of the canyon, the lifting of a head to behold the fullness of the dress. Without vision and breath, work has nowhere to go, nothing to accomplish. Clear vision and full lungs give strength and determination to an artist; they become a sort of faith that gives the work meaning. Work without faith is dead. The artist who knows what he is creating and why he is creating it possesses a flame that is very difficult to extinguish.

I am writing this book not as a philosopher of art, but as an artist. I'm a guy who creates things for a living. More specifically, I am a musician, so these things are most often made of frequencies and timbre, but I also dabble in words. I lead a musical collective called Güngör[1] and spend a lot of my time traveling around the world sharing our art with people. Much of the book is made up of my stories, and the ideas reflected in this book are admittedly subjective and rooted in my own artistic experience.

At times, I will also venture into areas that I would never claim to be an expert in—philosophy, theology, sociology, and so on. As you will eventually see, I hold most of my beliefs (even the serious ones) with loose fingers because I figure I am probably wrong about a lot of them. So when you come across these moments, think of them as playful jaunts intended to inspire and open the creative imagination to new ideas and possibilities, and not as dogmatic declarations of my less-than-qualified opinions.

It also might be worth mentioning that this book does include some adult language and stories that might not be appropriate for children. This may surprise some people due to the fact that my primary career is in composing church music, and many people like to imagine that church people don't say certain words or have genitals. I have no interest in trying to shock or be vulgar, but the way I see it, out of the nearly sixty thousand words in this book, it seems fairly natural that at least a few of them would have four letters. But if the idea of a church music guy dropping a swear now and then bothers you, please accept my humble apology and consider finding another book to read. There are lots of better ones out there anyway.

I tried to write this book with as few filters as possible, letting the words and ideas come straight from my humanity—warts and all. I tried to write this as honestly as possible because I believe that our art should be a direct expression of our humanness. Our art and our humanity are inextricably entwined, and within these pages, I hope to—through story and reflection—examine the soul-ish ground from which creativity arises.

---

1 Umlauts? My last name is Turkish, and the umlauts are normally included, but my American family doesn't use them, perhaps because they make the name look like a German death metal band.

I hope to assist in the opening of some head and heart space so that you, my fellow creators, can take inventory of your own manner of expression. I hope to help you step back and see more clearly what you are trying to do with your work.

So to those with weary and blistered fingers, this book is your invitation to hike with me back up to the ledge, take in the big picture, and remember who we are and why we do what we do. After we've remembered and drawn in a few deep breaths of that crisp desert air, may we be filled with courage to descend once more into the valley where the work gets done.

PART 1 ART

1. ART AND CREATION: SPEAKING THE LANGUAGE OF GOD

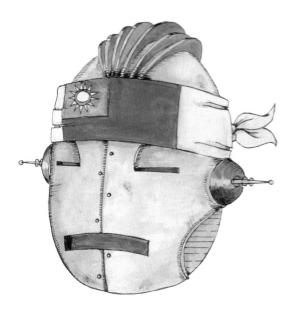

Art is the body's pronunciation of the soul.

Paint becomes an articulation of the painter's spirit—uttering his confessions in vowels and consonants of tea rose, sapphire, or deep chestnut formed into words that are faces and landscapes and abstractions. This is art.

The poet feels the pain or wonder of life pressing down on her chest and the breath that is forced out of her lungs is exhaled in iambic pentameter, haiku, or sonnet. Aimless, floating words are ordered with ink and imagination into epic, fable, free verse or limerick. This is art.

The industrialist sees his brother's need for warmth, shelter, tools, and so with his factories, fueled by sweat and ingenuity, he bends steel and mountain. In the furnace of his creativity, he melts raw potential, pouring it into the cast iron mold of intention, and it cools and hardens into his brother's met need. This, too, is art.

I will be writing of these things as a person who nearly flunked art class.

In junior high, I discovered that I had a unique and precise combination of shoddy craftsmanship, questionable aesthetic taste, and unimpressive visual intelligence that would never make me a great painter. This wouldn't have bothered me had I not been infatuated with the art teacher's daughter. But my chances with her dwindled as my brush shook in craggy lines across the page. I could sense the maternal presence lurking behind me—those judging, incredulous eyes fixed upon my work, which resembled the efforts of a much younger person, or perhaps a promising young chimpanzee.

In the meantime, my little brother, Rob, watched Bob Ross on public television and learned how to paint a landscape with some baby lambs roaming a field. My parents framed it. They still have it in their house. Honestly, I thought they made a bigger deal of it than necessary. *It was a freaking Bob Ross knockoff!* But that was all it took for the Gungor family to know who the most promising artist was in the family—and evidently, it wasn't me. I was more the bizarre, lanky, pseudo-afroed type whose artistic energy was poured into directing violent sci-fi home movies and trying to learn how to shred on an acoustic guitar.

I tried hard on a few of my art class paintings, but everyone seemed to think that I was only trying to be funny. So my defense mechanisms kicked in and I decided that if I was going to draw or paint something, the pictures would be absolutely absurd—sasquatches eating people, aliens with six giant breasts and so on.

The art teacher was not fond of my work.

Outside of the art teacher and her now-unattainable daughter, I didn't know many people in my town who were passionate about art. Surprisingly few of the great art collectors in the world choose central Wisconsin as their home. We may have lacked the so-called "culture" of modern art museums, poetry readings, or Shakespearian theater, but we did have the "World's Largest Round Barn," as well as an endless exhibition of farm smells, dive bars, and hundreds of thousands of pounds of white dimply fat.

I did know one other artist, though—my uncle from St. Louis. Man, I thought he was the coolest. His right hand's two middle fingers were mostly missing, so it looked like he was always making the rock-and-roll sign. He had a bit of a mullet and played a white bass guitar. As if that wasn't cool enough, he had a fridge full of beer in a pool table room that also featured a slightly abstract picture of a naked lady. He painted that picture, and I always hoped that the naked lady wasn't my aunt, because that would be super gross.

In my young, central-Wisconsinian mind, my uncle belonged to the world's small, elite group of Creative People who lived in big cities or college dorm rooms and spent their time doing impractical things like painting naked people or sculpting bowls. The artist was a romantic idealist who might weep at the sight of a fallen birch tree, but he wasn't someone who you would trust with your house keys. These kinds of people were interesting enough, but we didn't have much need for them in central Wisconsin.

For many people words like *art* and *creativity* feel lofty and out of reach. But in truth, the foundation of the artist's work is no different than any other human work. It's simply an intentional ordering of reality.

Every sentence you've ever articulated has been a creative work on some level. As a child, you learned how to use your tongue, lips and vocal cords to create sounds that have been culturally agreed upon to act as symbols of objects and feelings—even abstract ideas like justice or beauty. Speaking is the process of creating and communicating a series of thoughts by combining these sounds into patterns—like a painter combines individual colors into a painting or a musician strings together individual notes into a composition. Creativity is simply the human brain forming new connections between ideas, and we all are engaged in this process every day.

The common idea that there are some people who are creative and some who are not is a myth. On some level, we are all artists. We are all creators.

Of course, not all of us consider our work "art." Much human creativity gets ignored for the genius that it is because it so plain and practical. Take sewer systems for example.

We don't think of sewer systems as requiring artistic impulses. Nobody is painting sewer pipes different colors or experimenting with different finishes. Sewers are not intended as expressions of human creativity. They are intended to move our crap away to somewhere less intrusive.

But sewers surely are the result of creative genius. Somebody imagined them, designed them, and poured the cement for them. Did the designer of the sewer pipe not flex the same creative muscle as the painter or the poet? Does that sort of design not come from the same sort of brain activity, the same divine spark of humanness that is responsible for all design? Of course it does.

What we usually call "art" rarely has such specific and measurable goals. Often, it is simply creating for its own sake. But this does not mean that art is less practical than other work.

Art is Practical

I saw this most clearly a few years ago when Lisa and I traveled to Uganda. We were with a group visiting an orphanage that had taken in some of the children left in the wake of the civil war and genocide in Uganda's recent history. Our plan was to paint some murals at the orphanage. With my dearth of visual arts skills, I was not in the habit of volunteering to paint, but I figured I could at least help wash brushes or something.

As we drove to the orphanage, our heads jerking in unison at every bump of the pocked dirt roads, I remember noticing how plain everything was. The orphanage was a triad of little white structures that stood up in stark contrast to the ubiquitous reddish-brown dust that is the ground of Uganda—ground that looks like it has soaked up too much blood. Outside the sporadic greens of plants shooting up from the brown, or the backdrop blue of the African sky against the sheer white walls of the orphanage, there were few other colors in the bland landscape.

I was a bit jarred by such a lack of color. First-world cities like the one I live in are adorned with a million variegated tinges, a cluttered vivacity of endless billboards, SUVs, traffic lights, posters, and dumpsters. When people only make a couple of dollars a day, they don't have the luxury of aesthetic frills.

When we arrived, the children lined up and entered the room on their knees as a sign of respect. This was hard to watch. These children had lived through genocide, war and abuse. They had been abandoned and overlooked. They had seen violence and pain that no human being, yet alone child, should ever have to see. These kids were strong. They were survivors. Yet they bowed to us.

There is a story in the Bible about Jesus getting down on his knees and washing his own disciples' dirty feet. At first, the disciples feel really uncomfortable with the whole thing. I think I understand that now.

The children proceeded to put on a little show for us. They sang and danced, and when they were done, we picked up some guitars and sang for them as well. They laughed at our strange Western music, and we laughed at their laughter. When the singing was done, it was time to paint. I let the group know about my lack of skill, and I was instructed to just try to stay in the lines as best as I could. So we painted.

The murals weren't anything special. They were actually a little cheesy, like the kind of paintings that you see on the walls of nurseries and children's rooms in daycare centers or churches. But despite their lack of artistic sophistication, there was something important about bringing intentional color to those plain white walls. It felt like placing a crown on a beggar's head, yet somehow we also were the beggars receiving our own crowns in the process.

When we finished, the adults at the orphanage asked if we could use some of the leftover paint to cover a wall of the orphanage with the children's handprints. So we set up our paint by the white wall, and the children lined up politely to have their hands painted.

As orderly as they were behaving, when they reached the front of the line, palms up, you could see the thrill brimming from their smiles, threatening to burst beyond manners at any moment. They had never done any sort of art project like this, never experienced activities like "coloring" or "finger-painting," that I always took for granted as a child.

They held out their tiny hands to us, hands that had gone through far too much, and we slathered thick layers of primary color from fingertip to wrist. The children squealed in delight, laughing at the absurdity of such extravagance. We led them to the wall and helped them press their hands against it. Then we wrote their names under the tiny handprints, leaving a physical reminder to the world that these children were here, and they were loved.

It was surprising how drastically this small act of aesthetic intentionality changed the atmosphere of the orphanage. Those cheesy little murals brought color and life to a place that has been dry and barren and hopeless. Just as the barrenness had been expressed in the aesthetic of their surroundings, so these new colors were an expression of the love of those orphanage workers. They hadn't been able to afford paint, but they had believed that these children's surroundings mattered enough to invite a bunch of light-skinned foreigners to spend the day painting with them.

Our art, as insignificant as it seemed, spoke of value. Every brush stroke said, "You matter." Every handprint on that wall spoke of an orphan's humanity—her concrete existence in time and space. It was as if the cheap paint had somehow become the very colors of heaven splashed upon the longing surface of the earth.

This may sound exaggerated to those of us who live in a world filled with the aesthetic intentionality of landscaped yards and brushed silver spoons. But aesthetic beauty is a statement of value that makes the world a better place.

Art matters. It is not simply a leisure activity for the privileged or a hobby for the eccentric. It is a practical good for the world. The work of the artist is an expression of hope—it is homage to the value of human life, and it is vital to society. Art is a sacred expression of human creativity that shares the same ontological ground as all human work. Art, along with all work is *the ordering of creation toward the intention of the creator.*

My view of art, and consequently my expression of art, has changed quite a bit since my childhood in the Great North. I once saw art as an esoteric periphery to practical life—an elective, a hobby that sometimes becomes an obsession. Now I consider art to be an important, practical, and sacred part of human life. As a result, I take my art seriously. I compose music intended to open the heart. I spend a lot of time and energy crafting albums about big ideas like love and creation. I write liturgy for a community in Denver, Colorado, filled with weird, hippy, mountain people who seem to think that art is the language that God speaks.

For our community in Denver, this idea that we are all creators has become a sacred truth. Our creative expressions, whatever they are, have found deeper roots and meaning than mere ego expression or emotional gratification. We have found that the roots of our creativity go down deep into the soil of creation itself.

Creativity is a Gift

The archangel's flaming sword swung down and sliced open the box with the precision of a ninja and the power of a god. Trumpet fanfare erupted in the air as the curves of her jet-black electric body, the sharp angles of her rock-and-roll triangle headstock, and the glittering sterling steel whammy bar made contact with earth's air for the first time.

Actually, I was just opening one of those guitars that you can buy at department stores for $74.99, but to my ten-year-old eyes, this battle-axe was among the finest musical instruments ever crafted by human hands (or Taiwanese robots). Details like tone or intonation mattered little. All I needed to see was that name emblazoned in gold letters across the face of its headstock. This guitar had the best possible name that a boy could hope for. The name of the guitar was, of course, the *Terminator*.

The black T had a built-in amplifier. Did I mention that it was jet-black and had a triangle headstock that actually said Terminator on it? After I put the required 153 F-sized batteries into its back and cranked that built-in amp all the way up to ten, I felt like I could slay a dragon.

I would not be learning Bach preludes on the Terminator. I would not be practicing the changes to Moonlight Serenade. No, the Terminator was made for rocking, and it was made for rocking alone.

As an aspiring guitarist, I was dependent on the Terminator. All of my musical energy and creativity would now be flowing through its cheap strings and brittle tones. This is how human creativity works. It always depends on something else. Guitarists need guitars.

But the creative roots don't stop there. Nobody makes guitars from thin air. Guitars, like everything else, are made from things like trees and rocks and dirt. Clever people have figured out how to turn trees and rocks and dirt into black Terminator electric guitars, 747 jets, and laptop computers. From space shuttles to sculpted clay, all human creativity is an ordering of the potential already found within creation.

So I was dependent on the Terminator, which was dependent on the people who manufactured the Terminator. These manufacturers were not only dependent on all of the human creative genius that went before them in tempering music scales, creating musical theory systems, designing instruments, and so on; they were also dependent on creation itself. They depended on the potential within woods, metals, and sound waves. They (and the Taiwanese robots) drew them all together to make the Terminator.

All human creativity depends on something deeper than itself.

The frequencies of light that allow us to see the colors of the "Mona Lisa" were always there in the creation fabric, but it was not until human eyes and minds emerged from chaos, naming those frequencies "colors" and figuring out how to combine oils, milk, and chalk that the "Mona Lisa" could finally take its form. The universe was long pregnant with the potentiality of "Mona Lisa," but it was not until Leonardo da Vinci dipped his brush into this mixture of ordered creation called paint and brushed the precise possibilities of color onto a canvas made of some of earth's plants, that the famous, mysterious woman was able to take her form.

So where does it end? Where is the ultimate ground of art? The guitarist is dependent on the guitar, which is dependent upon the creation, which is dependent on whatever creative forces or realities are responsible for its existence. If you call this creative force or reality "God," then art really could be thought of as the language that God speaks.

All art is rooted in whatever is the foundation of *everything*.

Of course, people have always tended to get a little mystical about creativity. The ancient Greeks believed that human creativity came from goddesses that they called the Muses. These Muses were the source of all insight and knowledge. The Romans, on the other hand, believed that there was a divine nature at the heart of everything that they called the "genius." They believed this spark of the divine allowed men to create.

Today we have brain science that gives us insight into the nuts and bolts of creativity. We can see how the right hemisphere of the brain works to find unexpected relationships between seemingly disconnected ideas. We can put the brain in the scanner and watch gamma waves flicker across the computer screen as synapses fire and unite. Our scientific knowledge has progressed to the point that we don't need to attribute the finer tuned functions of the brain to gods or fairies with creative pixie dust.

Still, many of the greatest creators in our society have found it helpful to continue to speak in mystical terms.

Elizabeth Gilbert, author of *Eat, Pray, Love*, talks about a sort of creative Muse:

> I lifted my face up from the manuscript and I directed my comments to an empty corner of the room and I said aloud, "Listen, you thing, you and I both know if this book isn't brilliant that's not entirely my fault because you can see that I'm putting everything I have into this. I don't have any more. So if you want it to be better, you have to show up and do your part of the deal. But if you don't do that, you know what? The hell with it. I'm going to keep writing anyway because *that's my job*. And I would please like the record to reflect today that I showed up for my part of the job.

I've also heard this sort of thing in Christian circles. Only the creativity in those circles is not attributed to the Muses, but to God. A singer in a church might reply to a compliment with a phrase like, "Thanks, but it wasn't me, it was God."

Now, I am a bit of a romantic and perhaps even a mystic, but I'm not one to believe in goddesses that sit in the corner of the room while I write. And when I hear a singer attribute her performance to God, I have to restrain myself from saying, "Oh, well in that case, God was a little flat on that second verse."

But I do think there is something about a separation of the ego and the creative spark that can be helpful for the artist. Creativity is a gift. Whether the motor of human creativity is neurons and synapses or fairies and gods is beside the point. There are different ways of speaking of truth. In my faith tradition, God is seen as the ultimate creative source of all things, and I don't think that statement is in conflict with brain science. After all, my brain is not the source of itself and is dependent on a reality greater than itself. But whether the gift of creativity comes from God, evolution, or the Muses is, once again, beside the point. My point is that creativity is a gift that rises from deeper places than conscious thought—something that needs to be *listened to* rather than *forced* out of sheer willpower.

So when Elizabeth Gilbert talks about her Muse or a singer attributes her work to God, I think they are onto something. I find it inspiring to think that this Voice that the artist ought to listen to is the very voice of the Creativity that drew the universe into existence—the source of all creativity.

In the Beginning
The book of Genesis begins with a poem about a Creator who took a universe writhing in chaos and formed it into something cohesive, visible, and beautiful. When I was a child, I was taught that this poem was not a poem at all, but instead a literal, scientific depiction of the beginning of the universe. When I believed that, I never understood the genius of Genesis 1. But when I read it as a poem, it's more elegant, and it makes a lot more sense. When reading it as a poem, you don't have to worry about questions like, "But, wait . . . how could there be 'light' before there were stars, or night and day before an earth and a sun?"

It's a poem... I guess that's how.

In the Genesis story, humans become a part of this ongoing creative gesture that is the universe, and what sets us apart from the rest of creation is this breath that is breathed into dust. That breath is the image of the Creator. It is humanness, awareness, soul, spirit. It is a developed prefrontal cortex and the firing of unexpected synapses. Whatever you want to call it, it is what animates us. It is that thing that allows us to imagine, organize, create.

In Genesis, human creativity is a leathery truth. It's not abstract, groundless philosophical floatyness. It's breath meeting dirt. Flesh meeting spirit. It's not *ex nihilo*. It's an ordering of the chaos.

Some would say that this work of moving from chaos to order is the movement of God himself.

I am aware that even bringing up God in a discussion about creativity and art is going to alienate a lot of people. I understand that when I use the words "God" or "religion," many people will hear that which hinders creativity, progress, and great art. And when those words are used from a fundamentalist perspective, I would agree with them. Fundamentalism creates closed systems that are antagonistic to openness, imagination, or creativity. But I'm not using those words in that way. When I speak of God, I'm not speaking of some being *up there*. I am speaking of *Being* itself. Reality with a capital R.

I used to flirt with fundamentalism, and I had this idea that creation was something that *happened*. Now I see creation as something that is *happening*. Hundreds of millions of stars are still being born every day. Creation is an ongoing process. The Artist has not yet cleaned out the brushes. The paint is still wet. Human beings are the small clumps of clay and breath, and we have been handed brushes of our own, like young artist apprentices. The brushes aren't ours, nor the paint or canvas, but here they are in our hands, on loan.

What shall we make?

2. ART LIKE FRUIT: CREATIVE AWARENESS

Some witches wear snakes,
Some witches wear worms,
But I wear the Word of God.

--Michael Gungor's first musical composition, age three

And now, a pompous piece of art commentary:

In "Witches Wear Snakes in C Major," Gungor attempts to expose
the common superstitions within America's variegated forms of
religious expression by juxtaposing antiquated beliefs in witches

*and their serpentine ilk against the image of a fundamentalist
who "wears" his Scriptures as a sort of false self. The listener,
outraged, is provoked to exclaim: "What, then, is God?"*

In reality, I think I saw a cartoon where a witch had a snake wrapped
around her waist, and it horrified me. I mean, come on, are you kidding
me? A witch *and* a freaking snake? Terrifying.

At the time, I hadn't realized that the lyrics implied that *I* was a witch, but
such were the subtleties of lyricism that I hadn't quite mastered. As for the
last line about wearing the Word of God, I had been taught that the Bible
was a "double-edged sword." That sounded powerful. The song was an
attempt to convince myself that I didn't have to be afraid of witches with
snake belts because I had my Bible/sword that I could use to destroy them.

What kind of three-year-old thinks that the Bible is something he can use to slay witches? That assumption says a lot about the culture in which I was raised. If I had grown up in Richard Dawkins' home, perhaps I would have sang something more like:

> *All witches are fake.*
> *My knowledge is firm,*
> *Cause I know there is no God.*

Either way, I'd write and sing based on the world as it had been handed to me. I'd produce what I had been cultivated to produce.

Art is like fruit, and every tree is known by its fruit. Fruit reveals a lot about the tree from which it falls.

If you want to know what is in the heart of a man, don't listen to what he says. Look at what he does. A man can say that he believes in generosity. He can tattoo it on his chest and have it inscribed on his tombstone, but nothing speaks of his actual generosity more than how he spends his money.

If you want to know what is in the heart of a culture, look at its art. Read its poetry, listen to its music, and you'll begin to know the tree from which it fell.

Consider the music of the Middle East. This music often sounds strange and dissonant to the Western ear because of the way the scales are spaced out. The frequencies of the notes in these Eastern scales are closer together[1], which is why you often hear that dissonant, warbling effect in Middle Eastern music.

To some of you, all of this may sound like boring musical jargon, but the musical theory is actually very interesting when set against the political and social realities of the Middle East. I think it would be fair to say that

---

1 There are four half-step intervals in the Arabic scale as opposed to two in the major scale

this region of the world has gone through a lot of tension and conflict. It is, after all, the birthplace of the three major monotheistic world religions: Judaism, Islam, and Christianity. It's the region of the "holy land" that people have fought over for millennia. The Middle East has known war and turmoil for most of its history. In a nutshell, the culture is dissonant.

The music of the Middle East reflects this tension and dissonance. The fruit bears witness to the tree. The intervals bump against one another. The singing can sound like wailing, desperation, longing, pain, religious fervor. To hear Middle Eastern music is to hear the Middle Eastern soul.

In stark contrast, consider the music and culture of China. China is the largest nation in the world, and the Chinese are renown for their strict disciplines and social structures. For many years, the government in China has oppressed the artistic expression of the Chinese people. China has no freedom of speech or religion. For years, the Chinese people weren't even allowed to own musical instruments. The governmental policy in China has essentially been, "Fall into line, and don't mess with the system."

Chinese music is commonly built on a pentatonic (five-note) scale that is built in a way that creates the least amount of dissonance possible. In fact, unlike most other scales, you can play all the notes of a pentatonic scale at the same time without much dissonance[2]. In other words, the notes are so friendly with one another that you can cram them all into one tiny little space and they get along just fine.

This is all very Chinese. Over a billion people crammed into one nation will either find ways of aligning themselves alongside one another without too much dissonance or they will not exist as a nation very long.[3]

---

2   If you play all the notes of a C-major pentatonic scale, it actually makes up the chord known as a C6/9.

3   I've talked to different artists who have worked extensively in China, and apparently over the last five or ten years, things have been changing quite a bit. As doorways to the West have cracked open more and more, apparently many of the Chinese people are starting to branch out and appreciate other sounds and influences.

Our art does not exist apart from our values or philosophies; it does not transcend our views of God, the universe, or ourselves; it comes directly from them. Our deepest values and beliefs are like the root system of a tree. Everything we think, say, and create is filtered through them, influenced by them.

Yet, as creators we tend to be more mindful of the fruit than the tree. If the fruit is rotten, we tend to criticize the apple rather than looking at the branches from which the apple fell, the roots of the tree or the soil from which the tree draws nourishment.

An orange is an orange because it comes from an orange tree. Our art is the product of who we are. If we think the fruit needs to be sweeter, bigger, more nourished, we must pick up our watering can and pruning sheers and turn our eyes not just to the fruit, but to the very tree and its roots—to the soil that we are planted in and the nutrients that we draw our inspiration from.

The Critic
A few years ago, a formidable looking man approached me as I walked off of a stage. I thought I recognized him, but I couldn't remember from where. He shook my hand and told me his name. Then I remembered him. He used to volunteer playing percussion for me when I led worship at a church. I'll call him Johnson.

Johnson was part of the United States Special Forces, or Green Berets, the people that the military sends in for unconventional warfare, special reconnaissance, counter-terrorism, hostage rescue, and any other crazy stuff that no one else wants (or knows how) to do. . Johnson was also a decorated national war hero. He told me a story about how he had once broken his shoulder while parachuting into a secret mission. He jumped out of the plane and deployed his parachute, quietly sailing into the darkness. Then suddenly, he caught something out of the corner of his eye. A man. Dropping like a rock. Johnson saw the soldier drop past him and he knew something was wrong. Apparently the soldier had hit his head on his way out of the plane and knocked himself out. So Johnson, in a courageous act of heroism, took the knife out of his belt and cut his own parachute.

He dove headfirst through the sky without a parachute, trying to catch up to the plummeting, unconscious soldier. Somehow, Johnson reached him, strapped himself into the man's parachute, and managed to pull the cord and deploy the parachute just in time. Johnson broke his shoulder in the ordeal, but he saved that soldier's life.

In other words, Johnson is what the kids these days might call a BAMF.[4] As Johnson and I chatted at the side of stage, he told me that there was something he had wanted to talk to me about for quite awhile. While fighting in the Iraq war, he had been shot, and the doctors said that there was a strong possibility that he was going to die. He was in the hospital on what he thought was his deathbed. Johnson began to take inventory of his life, wondering if there was anything he needed to set right before he died. Was there any longstanding bitterness or anger? Anyone he needed to talk to before he died?

I felt sorry for that poor sap would be. Johnson is probably not a guy you want on your bad side.

He told me that there were two people that immediately came to mind. One was his father. They hadn't had a healthy relationship, and Johnson felt like he needed to humble himself and forgive his father. The other person he needed to forgive? Michael Gungor.

Excuse me?

That's right, little ol' me. Now, don't let my girlish figure fool you. I took Tae Kwon Do for a few years when I was a kid. I even won a prize for a

---

4   For the obscenity-averse, think of this as meaning "big as mother's flapjacks."

. . . well, you might call it a dance, but I would call it a dynamic, musical martial arts demonstration.

But even I, on my best martial arts day, would not have a prayer in defending myself against Johnson's special ops badassery. He could have picked any random hour that would have been convenient for him over the last decade to slip in a back door, window, or ventilation system to annihilate me in any way that he was in the mood for, and I could not have done anything about it.

I had no idea what I had done to provoke such long-standing bitterness in this very dangerous man.

So he told me the story.

One night at church several years ago, our drummer didn't show up, and everyone was scrambling and making phone calls to find somebody who could play for the service. Johnson was there that night, scheduled to play percussion, and he offered to play drums for us.

Now, just because someone can play percussion doesn't mean that he can play drums. Percussion is stuff like congas and shakers. Johnson had actually auditioned for drums in the past, but didn't make it.

Johnson told me that when he offered his services, I brushed him off with a casual "No, thanks." Apparently, in his ears, this amounted to something like, "Yeah, and I'm sure the ball boy would be happy to pitch an inning or two."

I told him that I didn't remember that story, but that I was sorry for being such a jerk. He laughed graciously and said that he had dealt with it already, and he knew I probably didn't even remember it, but he at least wanted to tell me and clear all of it from his heart and conscience.

I was thankful that he opted for that route rather than murdering me.

It seemed odd to me that this story would make the list of the most egregious offenses Johnson had experienced in his life. After all, someone had *shot* him. With a gun. There are a lot of people in this world that have literally tried to kill him. But apparently, these attempts on his life had not inflicted as much emotional devastation as my terse rejection of his drum-playing abilities at my church.

For the creator, there will always be *the voices.*

Voices of critique. Voices of affirmation. The voices of the ego and the audience. The marketers, the fans, the bloggers, or the executives. The more exposure that an artist has to the outside world, the louder the voices will become. The more successful the work, the more people will step in to try to influence and manipulate the work for their own benefit.

The creator has a decision to make.

What voice will I listen to?

This decision must be made daily. Hourly. Moment to moment. As the voices swell and pitch, demanding that she go this way or that, the creator must decide which voice to listen to.

The crowd, the critic, or the muse?

This decision will give her creation its form.

As strange as Johnson's deep offense may have seemed, I could relate. I have had enough experience with the voice of the critic to know how deeply it can hurt.

As a kid, I was a decent singer. I certainly was no "Star Search" contender (Crap, I'm getting old.), but I had a little raspy voice that some people found cute. Then puberty dawned its pimply little head.

It was time for the school play and I was given a solo. I was pretty nervous about it because my voice was starting to change from the cute little raspy boy voice to a lower, hormone-drenched, not-so-cute voice. The part of the song that I was slated to sing was a little too high for me, and the puberty problem was making it worse by the day. I tried to practice singing it down an octave, but that was too low. My range was just too small. I couldn't sing the song without some sort of unnatural vocal contortion, and as the date of the concert approached and my vocal chords stretched and hawed for stability, I grew increasingly worried.

The night of the concert, I still hadn't decided if I would try to belt it out high like Axel Rose or mutter it low and guttural like Johnny Cash. (Of course, I couldn't actually do either of these things.) This song had several featured soloists, and all of us stood in a line behind the microphone, waiting for our turn to show the world our talent.

I remember standing in line at the microphone, still unsure. It was almost my turn. What was I going to do? I guess I'd try for the higher octave, since a lot of the time I couldn't even get the lower notes to come out at all.

But then Banta sang.

My friend Ben, whom we all called "Banta," had gone through puberty faster and more effectively than me. His voice had already changed into a man's voice. He sang his lines low and confident. Before Banta, I felt okay about trying to sing the song in the girl range, but now Banta had ruined it for me. I couldn't sing like a girl after he had crooned the audience with his man-voice dripping with the testosterone created in his dropped man-testicles.

Freaking Banta.

It was my turn.

I went low.

Or, I tried to go low.

I opened my mouth to sing, but nothing would come out. It was too low. The music didn't wait for me, though, so I switched strategies mid-verse and shot for the high part. My voice cracked like the teenager who works at the burger joint on "The Simpsons."

I wanted to die.

As I struggled to find a note, any note, that could stay on the correct pitch for more than a millisecond, I felt every shred of my dignity and hope of manhood and musicality fade into the darkness of the auditorium. I stood there in the spotlight, exposed for the pathetic, greasy, zit-faced boy that I was. I hung my head in shame and walked back to the choir riser to a polite smattering of applause.

After the performance, I started hoping that maybe it wasn't as bad as I had thought. Maybe I had just exaggerated it in my mind.

Perhaps it would be one of those times when people say something nice like, "Oh, ninety-nine percent of the people out there didn't even notice!" That would have been great. But even if I couldn't find anyone to say that, I was sure to hear a few insincere "good job"s, and I would gladly take them.

Banta and I wandered out into the auditorium after the performance, and my eyes scoured the room, seeking affirmation. Normally, after children's plays, backs are patted, hugs and encouragement are given freely and liberally, whether merited or not. Normally. This time, no one seemed to be paying any attention to me. As I approached people, eyes curiously turned and other conversations were started.

I held out hope.

I saw my grandma approach.

Oh good! Even if it would be only a grandma compliment, which everyone knows is biased in the most extreme way possible, I needed it.

"Hi, Nana!"

"Why, hello boys!" she said to me and Banta.

I gave her a kiss on the cheek.

"My goodness, you did a great job tonight, Ben!"

"Thank you, Mrs. Gungor!" Ben replied in his polite and manly voice.

I waited for my compliment. It never came.

I couldn't get a compliment from my own grandmother.

That night, I decided to stop singing. After that concert, I didn't sing a note for anyone for four years.

Four years! She didn't even insult me. She just didn't compliment me. This is how fragile the ego can be in connection with our creative expressions. The critic's voice is so powerful because it resonates with the voices of our deepest fears, those voices speaking from inside of us, telling us that we are not good enough. The critics confirm our repressed and terrified suspicions that we don't measure up, that we are unsafe and unlovable.

We can hear "Bravo!" from ninety-nine voices, but they don't mean nearly as much as the "Eh" from the one. The voice of the critic can be like a hot dagger that reaches the heart quickly and surely. This is why Johnson took my snub to his deathbed. It really was more personally and emotionally painful to him than someone shooting at him in a war.

But the critic's voice is untrustworthy. Johnson probably heard things in my "no, thanks" that I wasn't trying to say. The voice that I heard that night from my grandma's lack of compliment said, "You are worthless as a singer. You should stop singing forever." In reality, what she was probably thinking was more like, "That performance was not very good. You need to work harder." Or perhaps, she didn't even realize that she hadn't said anything to me and didn't think much about it either way. But, whatever it was, I heard something else. This is how it works with the voice of the critic. It is untrustworthy—more is always heard than is spoken.

Creators are prone to listening too intently to the voice of the critic. We change ourselves and our art to please the critic so that we can feel safe, feel like we are worth something. But the critic doesn't care about your work in the same way that you do. The critic's voice is most often the voice of the preoccupied—a voice concerned with its own issues and its own ego. You are just a brief flicker on its radar screen. The voice of the critic is not sturdy enough to build your work on. It's too fickle, too fleeting.

On the other hand, the fact that the critic is not as emotionally invested in your work can actually make the voice of the critic quite helpful when listened to properly. The critic can help the artist see weaknesses and flaws in the work that the artist wouldn't have been able to see on his own. If my pubescent self had listened to the voice of the critic correctly, perhaps I would have practiced strengthening and growing more secure with my voice rather than just quitting for four years. If the heroic percussionist would have taken my declining his offer to play drums for me as an encouragement to get back into the practice room and work harder rather than being weighed down with a personal offense that he would take to his deathbed. Plus, I'm always in favor of nipping any sort of potential dead musician/incarcerated war veteran scenario right in the bud.

3. THE CROWD : ARTISTS LIKE QUESTION MARKS

The crowd is king.

–Josephus[1]

I have always found the psychology of crowds fascinating. Whether it's a town, an organization, or a neighborhood, crowds tend to develop their own personalities. The crowd's personality can often trump even the individual personalities of the people within the crowd. Groupthink emerges.

---

1   To the best of my knowledge, Josephus never actually said anything like this. Also, I'll try to limit the amount of untruthfulness in subsequent chapters. Thank you.

Groupthink is why people act differently at a sports event than they do at a classical music concert. Classical music lovers may be exhilarated about the second movement of "The Planets," but you'll rarely see a group of five shirtless guys at a Holst symphony with V-E-N-U-S painted across their chests. No, if the guys who paint letters on their chests at football games go to the symphony, they comb their hair, sit there in their suits and ties, and clap politely along with everyone else. All of us take our cue from the crowd on some level or another.

There are, of course those who tend to ignore the rules of the crowd—such as my brother Rob. Have you ever avoided reaching your hand into your popcorn during a silent or heavy moment in a movie so everyone doesn't have to hear you rummaging and crunching? For Rob, that's the perfect time to pull out his cell phone and use his fart app to fill the silence. Most people do not appreciate this sort of behavior. It seems people don't know what to do with loud and long flatulence during lulls in a dramatic movie. They just sit there in this offended, awkward silence. My dad shoots angry looks at Rob from the end of the row. Rob ignores him, sits perfectly still and expressionless, and pushes the button again.

Don't let the account of my dad's angry stares in the movie theatre fool you though. He and his Puerto Rican family are the one's who passed this penchant for the socially unacceptable down in the first place.

There are two reasons that most Puerto Ricans didn't migrate to central Wisconsin in the 1950s.

1. It is very cold there.
2. It is very white there.

Not many of them get to Chicago and exclaim, "You know what? Not cold enough. Continue northward!" But my Puerto Rican grandmother fell in love with a Turkish doctor (that's where the name Gungor comes from), and opted to move her family from New York City to the tiny, frigid, and racially monochrome Neillsville, Wisconsin.

My dad grew up not really knowing that he was a minority, so he was confused when people would yell at him from their cars, "Hey, bush nig***!" He was the closest thing to a black person in Neillsville, so he absorbed some of the racial tension of the day. He tells us he never thought of himself as anything but a white, rural Wisconsin guy, but when I see the pictures, his tight curly hair and classic Latino mustache beg to differ.

So of course people were a little suspicious when this smiley, afro-haired Puerto Rican guy who thought he was white ended up pastoring a Pentecostal church in rural Lutheran Wisconsin.

People generally keep a close eye on pastor's kids. They keep even a closer eye on kids like this:

Who are the offspring of guys like this:

I always felt watched. I was told that I was a representative of my dad, so my actions mattered, because people were watching. I didn't want to give him or the church he led a bad name, so I learned to keep my mouth shut. Life is easier if you don't offend people, and I learned how to be the polite, well-behaved pastor's kid waiting quietly in the corner of the room. For the most part, this approach served me well, though it has also kept me insulated from people. I still have a hard time being myself in certain situations.

I think this is why I enjoy people who are a little less sensitive to imposed cultural expectations—people like Rob or my wife, Lisa:

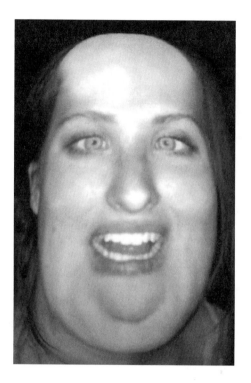

Isn't she lovely?

In real life, she actually is quite beautiful (before the Fat Booth and Bald Booth apps have digitally mangled her appearance), but there is something about this photo that somehow captures the essence of her personality quite well. What wife, after all, do you know that would allow her husband to post this photograph of her in his book?

If I err on keeping my mouth shut too often, Lisa makes up for it on the other side of the scale. If I am the quiet one sitting in the corner of the living room, Lisa is the one tap dancing on top of the table in the middle of the dining room. In our relationship, I'm the one giving the under-the-table leg squeeze when something inappropriate is said or done.

Lisa grew up as one of the only white girls in her New Mexico public high school. She was pretty, outgoing and just the right amount of sassy. When I met her, she kind of talked like she was a Mexican. It was confusing.

Lisa did not grow up worried about what religious people think. This becomes an interesting characteristic for a person that spends a lot time in churches. A couple years ago, we played a church gig that had all of the warning signs that we ought to really mind our religious p's and q's. There were pictures of pastors on the wall, and if there were a Güngör Church Behavior Rulebook, Rule Number One would say that if there are pictures of pastors on the wall, you shouldn't say the word "nipple" within five minutes of walking in the door.

Lisa hasn't read this imaginary rulebook as thoroughly as I have.

Here are a few more rules from the Güngör Church Behavior Rulebook:

> Rule 87: If you go into a church and see a lot of ties and mustaches (not hipster mustaches, but legitimate ones), use the term "bottom" rather than "ass."

> Rule 88: If a church has an American flag on the stage, do not mention that you voted for Obama.

> Rule 89: At dinner, never be the first one to order a beer.

> Rule 90: If the pastor orders a beer, you can get one, too— unless he has called you "brother," in which case he may be testing you. So order a Coke.

One of the first people that we talked to was the sound engineer. He came in wearing a tie, a short-sleeved dress shirt, and, of course, a thick pastoral mustache. He called himself Brother Something. I couldn't even keep track of all the rules in play at this point, but we were obviously in a religious taboo minefield. Best tread carefully.

"Hello, everyone, I'm Brother [let's call him] Steven. It's a blessing to have you. I'll be running sound for you, so please just let me know how I can serve you guys."

Before anyone else had a chance to respond, Lisa was in full swing: "Oh, hi! Yeah, is there any way we could move this keyboard a tid-nipple over this way?"

We all just stood there in silence. I couldn't understand why she would say that. Of all the phrases is in the world, she had to go right to nipples. I didn't even know what a tid-nipple was, but she was in clear violation of Rule Number One. Brother Steven just stood there, face flushed.

Lisa realized what she had said and started laughing. She was the only one.

As embarrassing as it can be to brave certain social situations with people like Rob or Lisa, it can also be incredibly inspiring to create with them. Our best creators will always be at least a little at odds with the crowd.

The crowd has its rules, and it will be very loud and adamant about these rules because without rules, the crowd's culture couldn't exist. But sometimes there are rules that ought to be bent or broken.

An argument could be made that you are not producing good art *until* you infringe upon some of your culture's rules and expectations. Perhaps artists in a culture are like prophets in ancient Israel, calling for society to repent and re-imagine itself. Artists like question marks, like incarnated doubt in the faith of a culture—keeping that culture fluid and growing.

All great human achievement or cultural advancement comes from people stepping out of the traditional and expected courses. The music that many of us love today never would have been created had not composers like Beethoven or Wagner broke the rules that had been set for them. This is how innovation works. Somebody breaks a rule and steps outside of the expected box. Eventually, that unexpected action becomes the new norm, the new box, until someone else comes along and breaks the new set of rules.

The role of the creator is an inherently precarious one. Somebody had to be the first person who proposed trying to build a ship that would fly to the moon. Walt Disney had to tell someone his dream of starting an empire based on a cartoon mouse. At some point in their lives, our most innovative creators get laughed at. They are scorned as fools, wastrels, or heretics.

In the middle of the nineteenth century in Europe lived a man named Ignaz Philipp Semmelweis. At this time in history, the mortality rate for women in childbirth was very high, and Semmelweis hoped to do something about it. He turned his attention to a clinic that had become notorious for its high percentage of women dying from puerperal fever after giving birth. The clinic's reputation was getting so bad that women would sometimes intentionally give birth in the street, then claim that they gave birth on the way to the hospital so that they could still receive benefits. They wanted to avoid giving birth in this death trap of a clinic.

Semmelweis noticed that the percentage of women who died of this fever was even higher for the women who gave birth in the clinic then it was for those who gave birth on the street. He was determined to find out how this could be.

In his research, he discovered that many of the doctors delivering these babies were also routinely handling corpses.

Eventually, he came up with an idea—one that would change the world, saving countless lives, eradicating certain kinds of diseases, and making life better for millions of people.

What was Semmelweis' brilliant insight? He suggested that doctors wash their hands after handling the corpses.

That's it.

That was his revolutionary idea. This, of course, sounds like an obvious solution to those of us living in the twenty-first century with the luxury of knowing about things like germs and bacteria. But in Semmelweis' day, people didn't wash their hands like we do now. Semmelweis might as well have been demanding that everyone clean their ears and hop up and down three times after every surgical procedure. People thought he was crazy. He ended up being committed to and dying in a mental asylum. The creator shouldn't always listen to the voice of the crowd.

Of course, there will be times when the voice of the crowd should be heeded. It is the crowd that gives the artist her language, her tools, her mode of expression. The voice of the crowd can teach the artist how to speak more effectively with her work. Without a culture, the artist has no language and no one to speak to.

But the voice of the crowd will never lead the creator to step outside of the crowd's expectations. The crowd will always demand the expected and controllable. And the plain truth is that the crowd is often wrong. Sorry Josephus, the crowd is not always king.

Navigating the Voices
The band was getting dressed in the green room, getting ready to go out on stage, when our road manager approached me with a concerned look.

"Okay, Michael, I've got something crazy to tell you."

"Your physical attraction to me has gotten out of hand?"

"Yes, but we'll talk about that later. No, I got a text from _____, and apparently the president of the radio station that is promoting tonight's show wants you to play 'Wrap Me In Your Arms.'"

"'Wrap Me In Your Arms'? Why? That's such an old song . . ."

"I don't know, he likes it for some reason. Anyway, here's the crazy part: He's coming to the show tonight just to see if you will play it. And if you don't, the radio station is never going to do anything to promote Güngör again."

"What?! Did he really say that?"

"Yeah, they basically are threatening you. What do you want to do?"

All the voices began speaking at once.

You see, the radio station promoting our show that night is one of the biggest and most influential stations of its type in the whole country. Hundreds of radio stations all across the nation take their cue from this station's decisions. To have their support is extremely advantageous, and to be on their blacklist is no good.

There was potentially a lot of money at stake. If I complied, there was a chance to gain some influence and powerful alliances.

On the other hand, the set we were playing had been designed as a complete narrative told through four very intentionally composed movements, and "Wrap Me In Your Arms" didn't fit with the art we were creating that night.

The voices started arguing.

One part of me felt a swell of pride. *Who does this guy think he is?*

My ego spoke up, wanting me to demonstrate to everyone that I am a strong, virile man.

Like a tiny cartoon devil on my shoulder, it whispered into my ear: *Do you really want to look like a pushover in front of everyone? What do you think the musos will think of you for playing an old, cheesy song like that?*

But I heard another voice whispering in my other ear: *What's the big deal? You did help write the song. And the radio station has been helpful to us. Would you really want to say no to this powerful radio station? Some money and influence wouldn't hurt you right now.*

This gave the first devil pause, because my ego is drawn to things like money and influence. (They give people the impression that I am a strong, virile man.)

Other voices chimed in. The critic said I was a sellout for even considering playing the song. Older fans said Güngör has gotten too artsy and needs to get back to the basics.

I could hear the voice of the industry. *Play the song!*

I could hear the voice of my friends. *Don't play the song!*

The marketers. *Play the song!*

My manager. *Don't play the song!*

The voices blurred into a loud grey static. I told my road manager that I needed to step outside for a minute. I tried to find the quietest place possible because I knew that there was a voice inside of me that would be speaking the correct answer, but I couldn't hear it in all of the noise.

Sure enough, after a few minutes of quiet, an answer presented itself.

I was thankful for the radio station's support, so I would say it. I would thank them from the stage. I also was able to see that a decision to do that song would come from only negative motivators—fear, greed, social jockeying. I could not play the song for the sake of art. I could not play it out of love or honest expression. To play the song would be to simply kiss the ring of this guy whose favor I longed for. (Plus, I've heard that you should never try to negotiate with terrorists.) So, I decided not to play the song.

I don't tell you this to try to make myself into some kind of artistic hero or something. I'm not. As a creator, I have made plenty of dumb decisions, kissed the king's ring, and acted out of fear rather than courage or love more than I care to admit. But when I do have the clarity of mind and heart to actually *make* a creative decision rather than just stumble into an instinctual one, I have learned over the years that it is far better for me to follow my gut and conscience more than my fear. Fear leads to burnout and death, but the Voice inside always leads to life. Following that voice may not always lead you to fame or riches, but it will lead you towards creating in a way that is consonant with your soul.

The external voices can be helpful for the creator, but they can never tell her who she is. The voices of the crowd or the critic can help us become more self-aware, more inspired, and provide channels to share our work with the world. But these external voices can never be the primary source or inspiration for the creator. Creative work should not come out of who the external voices want you to be, or who you wish you were, but from who you *are*.

You are not a mere cog in a machine. You are a human being, unique and miraculous. The whirls and lines in the skin of your fingertips are unique to you. Only you have your particular set of relationships, beliefs, passions, and circumstances, and only you have the ability to create what you ought to create.

As an artist, the voices you listen to ought to align with that inner Voice that knows who you are. When that foundation is set, then the rest of the voices can begin to build and work together, becoming the voice of a community, adding synergy and depth to your art that you couldn't possibly manufacture on your own. Of course, this sort of harmonization demands a level of awareness that most of us don't normally operate from.

Name Deafness

The town in Wisconsin that I grew up in was called Marshfield. If I hadn't already made it clear, you could probably derive from the name *Marshfield* that my hometown is not an epicenter of national cultural influence. When I hear "Marshfield," though, I hear something different than you do. Sure, "marsh" + "field" seems to describe an expansive swampland. But when I hear those words combined, I hear the home of my childhood. I hear the sound of riding my bike downtown as a ten-year-old without fear of strangers. I hear the little shop that I used to trade baseball cards at, the frigid public pool, and the late night conversations with friends at Perkins Family Restaurant.

In my ears, "Marshfield" sounds like simplicity and innocence. Others may hear it more literally—and maybe more correctly—but I'm deaf to all that.

There are towns in Pennsylvania called Intercourse, Virginville, and Blue Ball. It's true. Oh, and be sure to visit the Intercourse Pretzel Factory next time you are in Intercourse—I hear they make a mean pretzel.

Scotland is home to both a Backside and an Assloss. Did the founders of Townville, South Carolina fail to see the redundancy? Do the people who live in Boogertown, North Carolina ever think of voting for a name change? Do the people who live in Euren (pronounced "urine"), Wisconsin or in Goochland County, Virginia ever wonder why? Probably not—all these towns are likely inhabited by people whose love of and familiarity with the towns make the names beside the point.

My mother's maiden name is "Griesbaum" (pronounced "grease-bomb"). I have never heard any of the "Bomber Girls," as the Griesbaum daughters were often called, bemoaning their ridiculous last name. They aren't concerned that their surname's syllables can be broken up into words used as a potent epithet for flatulence: "Damn, who dropped a grease bomb?" The Bomber Girls and Bomber Bros don't hear that when they hear "Griesbaum." They hear mom and dad. They hear bombastic voices bellowing carols around the Christmas dinner table. They hear home and belonging. They hear family.

When something is as close to you as your own name, you see it, hear it, and understand it differently from everyone else.

Human beings are inherently subjective creatures. It's impossible to see without using *your* eyes. We live, love, work and create according to beliefs and values that are entrenched so deeply in us that we may not always recognize them. Our ordering of creation doesn't just come from our conscious imagination, but is colored with all of the subtext and buried assumptions and beliefs of our subconscious that has been subjected to endless cultural conditioning from the time we were born.

As I have traveled more and more over the last few years, I've often become aware of my own cultural conditioning—often in the most mundane and unexpected places like standing in line (How close do you stand to the person in front of you?) or sitting at a dinner table (Should you use your hands or the utensils?).

I was at a Christian event in Germany recently and a young man wanted to take a photo of me. He politely asked if I could move over a little because there was a "f***ing light" behind me. I feel the need to put those asterisks in there because in the culture that I spend a lot of time in (and that many of my readers probably inhabit), the specific combination of sounds that are represented by the letters in that word is considered socially taboo. Have you ever wondered why that is? Most of us don't really think about that. We just know that it is. Those sounds are *bad* in our culture. But they obviously don't bother that Christian guy in Germany. He has experienced a different cultural conditioning that probably makes different words feel *bad* to him—sounds that would make him gasp would mean nothing to those of us who don't speak German.

Our cultural conditioning is so ingrained in us that we often see these customs and taboos as inherent to the fabric of the cosmos. We spiritualize them. Legalize them. And when someone else doesn't follow them, it can feel to us like an attack on our very personhood. This kind of cultural blindness affects how we order creation.

Creativity generally involves a lot of gut reaction and instinct, and many of these feelings are rooted in our cultural conditioning. The songwriter doesn't necessarily choose a particular lyric because it is the most reasonable or grammatically sound, but because it feels good. The average listener doesn't like a song because of the complex rhyme scheme or interesting mathematics that lie behind the harmonies. She likes it because of the emotions it stirs inside of her. But if we never step back and wonder why something makes us feel the way that it makes us feel, we are stumbling in the dark. Many creators become prisoners of their own emotions and instincts, blind to what is influencing them. Without some level of both self-awareness and cultural awareness, artists can easily become artistically imprisoned as mere products of their environment—the fruit of a cultural tree.

This might not be a major problem if the cultural tree is robust and healthy. But this, of course, is a rarity.

As I write this, the number one song in the country is "Sexy and I Know It." The song has an upbeat tempo of 130 beats a minute, which is pretty much the standard for pop hits right now (see appendix 1). The harmonic structure of the song consists of one minor chord. The instrumental textures of the song consist of a synthesizer. The lyrics consist of a first-person narrative about a man walking around in a Speedo telling everyone how sexy his body is.

In the music video, the viewer is treated to visual surprises like close-up shots of wiggling male genitals outlined in flashy Speedos while the artist enthusiastically exclaims, "Wiggle, wiggle, wiggle, wiggle!"

The song has a catchy melody, and the irony of the artist's outlandish singing about his sexiness is admittedly pretty funny. Good beat, fun song—no surprise that it would sell. But it isn't just *selling*. It is the top-selling piece of music in the whole country. Of the millions of songs recorded in the history of the world, including the musical genius of Mozart, John Coltrane, or the Beatles, the group LMFAO (which is an acronym for "laughing my f***ing ass off") is selling the most.

This is the art that our culture is giving rise to.

It's reasonable to speculate that "Sexy and I Know It" wouldn't have been a number one song in decades past. I have a hard time imagining my grandparents swing dancing to Glenn Miller one moment and thrusting their hips to "wiggle, wiggle, wiggle" the next.

"Sexy and I Know It" is the number one song for a reason, though. The music of LMFAO has something to tell us of the humanity that creates and consumes this kind of art. This is the culture that provides the nourishment for our creativity. Even those who may not enjoy LMFAO or any of the most popular artistic expressions of the day should not fool themselves into thinking that the culture that gives rise to LMFAO has no effect on them. Art is always connected to the culture of the artist.

When so much of the cultural fruit around us is meager and mealy, it is important for the creator who desires her work to develop into something more substantive and nourishing to develop a healthy awareness of what is guiding her creative impulses.

Art doesn't necessarily need to be self-aware to be a viable and valuable human expression, but without self-awareness, the artist has very little ability to change or improve the nature of his work. He becomes imprisoned by whichever course his animal instinct wants to take. He simply responds to whatever is the loudest voice in his subconscious. As creators, we ought to learn to open our eyes to our very eyes—to look at the very mechanism of looking that we have grown accustomed to. With awareness, we are able to recognize and use these voices to our advantage. We can recognize and utilize our instincts and cultural conditioning to transcend the beaten path and move toward creative freedom.

In the next part of this book, I'd like to take a look at six specific social realities that heavily influence our culture and its creative expressions. These realities are like roots that feed and support the cultural tree that gives rise to our creative expressions. These roots go deep in the American soil, lying at the heart of much of our work and artistic expression.

The six roots are:

1. Noise
2. Technology
3. First World Mindset
4. Capitalism
5. Celebrity
6. Religion

While other cultures throughout history have drawn from these same roots, contemporary American culture has done so in a unique and powerful way. Non-American cultures draw from these roots, too, but I'll focus on American culture because, well, I am an American, and like Mark Twain said, "Write what you know."

Before I close this chapter, I do have one final observation to make. It has to do with the Griesbaums.

The Griesbaums happen to have a cemetery plot next to another prominent St. Louis family who are coincidentally good family friends of theirs. I promise you that I'm not making this up—there is a St. Louis cemetery where the Griesbaums are buried next to the Greasydicks.

No comment.

PART 2 ROOTS

4. NOISE: FAT KIDS AND PIANO CONCERTOS

Whoa, that's a full rainbow. All the way.
Double rainbow. Oh my God.
It's a double rainbow all the way.
Whoa, that's so intense.
Whoa, man, Wow.
Whoa, whoa, whoa oh, oh, oh, oh! OH!!
Oh my God!! OH MY GOD!!
WOOO!!!! WOOOOOOW!!! WOOOOOH!!!! YEAH!!!!! Oh!!
Oh my!! [starting to cry]
It's starting to look like a triple rainbow.
Oh my God, it's full on!

Double rainbow all the way across the sky!
Oh my God!! [weeping now]
What does this mean?

--Double Rainbow Guy[1]

One of my all-time favorite pieces of music is the second movement of Rachmaninoff's "Piano Concerto No. 2 in C Minor."

The movement starts with this crescendo of chords that the strings and woodwinds play together, but then fades to the pianist, who takes center stage in this composition. He begins to arpeggiate a progression of chords that always stirs something in my soul. It's fascinating to me how certain combinations of sounds can carry such emotional weight. What is it, after all, that makes a minor chord feel more melancholy than the "happy" major chord? It's amazing to me that by simply lowering the third of the chord a half a step, the composer can create an entirely different emotional response in the listener.

Rachmaninoff juxtaposes a set pattern over different types of chords that share unique relationships to one another. The effect in me is as if each chord reaches a new place in my soul, but doesn't stay in one spot for long. It is a stirring.

What is it, exactly, about the just-right combination of wooden hammers striking metal strings that bring tears to my eyes?

There are some things about the music that I do understand. I have the ability to understand the mechanics of it. I can rationally analyze the theory of its composition. But the music carries something heavier on its wings than math or mechanics—something like stories and kisses and color. There's something that seems to lie just beyond the actual frequencies and timing of notes that speaks of a sort of transcendence.

---

1   If you don't know who this is, just ask Harvey YouTube, and thank me later.

Maybe this is what C.S. Lewis was talking about when he wrote in *The Weight of Glory*:

> The books or the music in which we thought the beauty was located will betray us if we trust to them; it was not in them, it only came through them, and what came through them was longing.

> These things—the beauty, the memory of our own past— are good images of what we really desire; but if they are mistaken for the thing itself they turn into dumb idols, breaking the hearts of their worshippers.

> For they are not the thing itself; they are only the scent of a flower we have not found, the echo of a tune we have not heard, news from a country we have never yet visited.

Somehow, when I listen closely to Rachmaninoff, I feel the presence of that country that sends its notes ahead of the time of its becoming in the form of a dozen violinists coordinating their movements so that their bows uniformly and gradually increase in pressure, rousing the strings to become a voice in the swell of sound that underscores the piano's hypnotic arpeggios, and the splendor that lies hidden in ink and lines rises to take its form.

Listening intently, I imagine the conductor—the slow dance of his arms aligning the inner clocks of every musician and listener to his own. He leads the musicians through the maps of manuscript paper, staves and dots that speak of precise shapes and rhythms of lips and fingers. Every individual mind in the orchestra is primarily engaged in the details of his/her own specific part, yet, somehow, all of the pieces melt into a single cohesive and magnificent whole. This music carries beauty on its back with ease.

When I listen, I mean really *listen*, there is so much to hear—subtleties of tone and color, motif and countermelody.

But when not fully attended to, the richness of Rachmaninoff becomes the more generic "classical music," like looking at the faces of a crowd rather than the face of a person. When played too quietly or peripherally, classical music tends to dull into a vague but formal stuffiness. If I play music as background noise, I do not really hear it.

If I don't really listen, I could never hear the coughs of the audience, pianist Van Cliburn's sharp intake of breath, or the roundness of the horn's tone. All of this is part of the humanness of the music, but you cannot hear these things when the music hides in the background. I love to listen to this kind of music sitting in front of a fireplace or underneath the stars with my best headphones on, doing my best to hear what I can, waiting for beauty to enflesh itself in sound. I turn up the music loud because I want no other sounds or voices to compete with it. I want to be fully present and attentive to the potential echo of Beauty herself.

Most people don't listen to music like this anymore.

The world is too loud. We have too many competitors for our attention. Political voices, religious voices, educational voices, bosses, employees, hectic schedules, and aggressive marketers. We are overstimulated.

Here is a snippet about marketing from a recent CBS story:

> "Well, it's a non-stop blitz of advertising messages," president of the marketing firm Yankelovich, Jay Walker-Smith, said. "Everywhere we turn we're saturated with advertising messages trying to get our attention."

> Walker-Smith says we've gone from being exposed to about 500 ads a day back in the 1970s to as many as 5,000 a day today.

> "It seems like the goal of most marketers and advertisers nowadays is to cover every blank space with some kind of

brand logo or a promotion or an advertisement," Walker-Smith said.

Marketers have found a way to use parking stripes, postage stamps and floors, even buses and buildings, like a target ad which practically engulfs an entire New York city block. Walker-Smith says it's all an assault on the senses.

Of course, as I read this article on my computer, I had to close the floating pop-up windows obscuring the text. Ironically, this web page decrying the "assault on the senses" was plastered full of distracting advertisements and manipulative marketing.

The world is getting so loud. We are overstimulated. Numb. Bored. This is why most current popular songs are only three or four minutes long—we don't have the attention spans for anything longer than that. This is why there are so many music videos with pimped-out cars and dancing girls in bikinis.

It is the same reason that grocery stores put gossip magazines and candy bars in the checkout aisles. Few people go to the supermarket for the primary purpose of buying candy bars, but when you are there waiting in line, that candy bar can look pretty tasty, as does the latest morsel about Brad and Angelina. The marketers count on earning your dollar at that moment not by targeting your rational mind with reasoned arguments, but by appealing to your baser instincts.

Most popular art is like candy and gossip magazines. It is not meant to provide substance, but to grab our attention. It tastes really sweet, and makes us feel good for a moment. But if all you eat is candy, it'll eventually take a toll on your health.

Fat Kid

When I was a kid, my dad always used to tuck me in and give me a kiss goodnight. One particular night, I had already fallen asleep before he came in. When he finally entered the room and leaned over me to kiss my cheek, he smelled something minty. He looked at my face and saw my cheeks puffed out like a half-Puerto Rican chipmunk. He had made the peculiar discovery that his sleeping boy's mouth was full of Mentos, *The Freshmaker*.

This is the perfect example of what some might call a "fat kid moment."

I have always had quite the sweet tooth.[2] If you checked my pants pockets at any point before I was twenty years old, you would have had a seventy-four percent chance of finding at least one Butterfinger wrapper. One time, my wife was moving my coat and she felt something stuck inside. She pulled, but it was stuck pretty good. She finally got it out, and to my shame and her amusement, it was a caramel dipping sauce container from McDonald's. It had gotten stuck to the liner of the back of my winter coat.

Fat.

Every fat kid knows that eating too much candy will eventually take its toll. If you sleep with Mentos in your mouth, your teeth are going to rot. If you chew on an entire package of sour gum balls in one sitting, your tongue is going to hurt the next day. And if you spend a lot of time reading gossip magazines, you may find Shakespeare doesn't pop like the *National Enquirer*. If you listen to hours of pop music every day, you may find yourself getting bored during the development of Mahler's themes.

I had to slow down on the sweets when I got to college because my six-pack was devolving into a keg. Part of the problem was that my stupid friend Andrew told me about this new fat-free custard stand in town. The custard was amazing, and I ate it every day. I soon began to wonder why

---

2 In editing the book just now, I was reading this part out loud to my wife, who pointed out that I had a cherry sour ball in my mouth.

my ass was getting so large. The custard that I had been consuming by the gallon was not fat-free by any stretch of anyone's imagination. Freaking Andrew. He's the pastor of the church that we are a part of now, and I know him well enough to realize that he probably told me about the fat-free custard just to mess with me.

There are consequences when you pound down gallons of custard and sleep with Mentos in your mouth. Eventually, you start getting fat. Your taste in food changes. Your health starts to decline.

Behold: pop culture.

The fruit speaks of the tree. Today, most of our cultural fruit is infected with the (probably accurate) assumption that consumers will not appreciate depth, complexity, or honesty as much as a quick distraction. We want explosions, not character development. We want something to grind to on the dance floor, not something to provoke reflection. Artists respond to our desires, and they've little incentive to delve into deep artistic labyrinths of beauty and complexity. Who would buy it?

We consume our art like moths. We gather, momentarily, around wherever the biggest, brightest light seems to be. So these days, the most successful art is the art that can elicit the quickest visceral reaction from the largest group of people.

This is why sex sells so well. Sex is a very bright light.

Imagine that you are seated in front of two screens, each playing a music video. The first video contains a contemplative piece of music playing underneath slow-moving images evoking the nature of human suffering. The second video shows Katy Perry taking her clothes off. Which screen do you think you are going to be prone to look at?

Sex sells. Shock sells. Bigger and brighter and louder sells. And they don't just sell—they ensure that our imaginations fall into disuse.

The Riot of Spring

Consider this true story from an era before smartphones or PlayStations—the early twentieth century:

It was a pleasant spring evening in Paris, May 1913. The brilliant Russian composer Igor Stravinsky was debuting his new composition, "The Rite of Spring." The work was set to a ballet—common fare in the Paris of the time, but the attendees that night had no idea what was in store for them. From its title, "The Rite of Spring" sounds genial, but it refers to a ritualistic pagan murder that the dancers enact at the end of the piece. Both the choreography of the ballet dancers and the tonality of the musical composition would be unlike anything anyone had ever seen or heard.

The piece begins normally enough, with a lovely melodic passage played on a bassoon. Soon, this pleasant melody gives way to a darker dissonance, and tension begins to build as the other woodwinds tiptoe into the sonic soundscape. What begins as something like the sound of a lovely spring day becomes tinged with a sense of foreboding.

Around the three-minute mark, the piece takes an unexpected turn. The orchestra erupts into a wildly dissonant polychord, played in a sharp, stabbing rhythmic pattern. This early in the twentieth century, any chord containing such fierce dissonance would have usually been resolved fairly quickly into something more palatable to the ear. But Stravinsky doesn't do that.

When Sergei Diaghilev, the director of the Ballet Russe, first heard this chord as Stravinsky played the piece for him on the piano, he asked the composer, "How long will it go on like that?" Stravinsky looked up at him and replied, "To the end, my dear."

Stravinsky wasn't kidding; the dissonance just stays, jarring the listener's ears over and over again. The listener is immersed in the tension that builds while the chord repeats itself again and again without pause or change.

To our contemporary ears, "The Rite of Spring" may not sound all that outlandish. In fact, it was later enjoyed by children all around the world in the 1940 Disney animated film, *Fantasia*. At the time, however, no one had ever heard anything like it. On that Paris night in May 1913, as the orchestra played that same unresolved chord over and over again, people began to get uncomfortable. The dissonance just sat heavy in their ears, a brooding score to the ballet dancers' unconventional tribal-like movements across the stage. The tension in the room finally snapped, and all hell broke loose.

A riot ensued. People screamed and booed. Old ladies struck one another with their canes. Fistfights broke out in the aisles. Stravinsky reportedly watched the mass chaos, and then fled the stage in tears.

Can you imagine such a thing happening at a ballet performance today? Perhaps if the material was controversial enough, you could get an audience to boo and maybe even leave, but a full-out riot? Can you imagine people today experiencing such a fierce emotional response to a piece of music that they would actually start punching people around them?

What must those people have been feeling to *actually riot*? This was no polite dismissal: *That music is just too dark for me*. No, we are talking about white-hot blinding rage! Have you ever experienced an emotion that strong from listening to music? How many of us today listen to the sounds and subtleties of music close enough to be able to feel anything resembling that amount of emotion?

The audience of that time did not see hundreds of thousands of advertisements a year. They didn't watch thousands of commercials with beautiful, digitally enhanced people selling products that pop onto our screens with catchy music and special effects. They had never seen the giant U2 claw/stage, Lady GaGa's meat dress, or James Cameron's impressive 3D depiction of a lush alien planet.

The world wasn't quite as noisy in 1913. Back then, when people went to listen to music, they actually listened to the music. There were no light shows to distract them. There were no motion or video backgrounds, audience blinders, or lasers. They just sat there and listened to musicians play music, letting the sounds wash over them completely. They watched ballet dancers dance and felt the movements. They felt it in the core of their being—so much that they could be moved to the point of riot. And if they felt rage, what other emotions must they have been able to experience? What degrees of joy, serenity, longing, or hope did these people feel when attending to art with full attention and open hearts?

Things have changed.

Emotron

Amie was one of the first friends Lisa and I made when we moved to Colorado. Amie is a bit of a hippie.[3] She lives in an old school bus that has a wood-burning stove. She spends her summers in places like India or the Burning Man festival. And she has very interesting friends.

The first time we hung out with Amie, she took us to a party at a hippy commune. All of the hippies lived in this house together, and the house did not smell good. But it seemed to work for them. The hippies wandered around, sipping wine or homemade beer and snacking on food that looked like hay and purple mush. Musicians set up in the back yard where they would be performing for us to the chagrin of the neighbors, and eventually the police. Little did I know at the time that the performance that was about to happen in the hippies' backyard would be among the most memorable concert-going experiences of my life.

There were several bands that played that night, but the artist that really sticks out was Emotron, a man we first saw when he sauntered into the backyard in full John Wayne apparel. Cowboy hat, boots, chaps, and so on. He looked like he was in his twenties, but he wore these big, thick old

---

3   And James Earl Jones is a bit of a black man

man glasses. It was an odd look, especially for a party full of hippies. Was this guy a cowboy? A hipster? A homeschooler? As we would soon find out, though, Emotron transcends categories.

For instance, one might expect a man dressed in country western clothes to pick up an acoustic guitar and play some country western songs. Not Emotron. In fact, Emotron would not bother with unnecessary musical shackles like instruments or melodies. He would be performing strictly to tracks. The music on the tracks sounded kind of like those demo songs on Casio keyboards. But that didn't matter. Emotron's show wasn't primarily about the "music."

What Emotron may have lacked in wardrobe taste, musical quality, or lyrical subtlety (foulest lyrics you've ever heard; absolutely filthy) he made up for in passionate performance. He was at 100% from "Go." The Coke-bottle-spectacled cowboy screamed to his haphazardly-produced keyboard track, running back and forth in the hippies' backyard as though he were a rock star on speed running across the stage of a stadium packed full of screaming fans while simultaneously being attacked by a swarm of bees. He was exerting more energy in this backyard performance than I have ever seen anyone exert on any stage.

In the middle of the first song, Emotron threw off his cowboy hat and revealed a curious but classic bald man hair donut. Only, it looked a little strange. Too thick on the sides or something. I looked at Lisa, whose mouth was wide open in amazement.

"Is that real, or do you think he just shaves it like that?"

"It looks shaved to me."

"Right? But why would someone do that?"

"Why would someone do this?"

I looked back. He was now removing his clothing. Underneath his cowboy suit, he had a zebra-striped leotard on.

The sight of this wannabe balding cowboy (we found out later that he had been cutting his hair like that for years) with his huge old man glasses frolicking around the backyard of the commune and screaming his obscenities in a striped leotard was just too much. Lisa and I were cheering and laughing our guts out.

At some point, we both realized no one else was laughing. All of the hippies were just nodding and watching Emotron as seriously as if Maya Angelou was reciting poetry in the backyard. The world had evidently stopped making any sense.

The next "song" started, and Emotron began to remove his costume again. Under the zebra leotard, he wore a pair of short purple spandex pants. During this song, he would jump into the air and land flat on his back in a very painful-looking land flop. After every back flop, he would jump right back up to his feet and continue running around, occasionally stopping to make himself gag by sticking his fingers down his throat. He was trying to make himself throw up, but having a tough time of it, apparently. I looked back and forth from the gagging Emotron to the serious-faced hippies, and it was all so surreal.

At the end of that song, he began his now customary costume removal, thanked the audience, and said that this would be his final song. This time, the costume was nothing but a tiny pair of neon-green briefs with the head of a baby doll glued to the crotch.

While Emotron gyrated in his tiny and obscene costume, I turned to Lisa and made a comment about how I was glad it was his last song, because there was nothing left to take off.

I was wrong.

A few seconds later, the briefs came off.

Lisa's scream alleviated my fears that perhaps I had lost my mind. She was seeing this, too. So the hippies had not drugged me. I was not seeing things. That scrawny, bald-headed guy screaming to the Casio track was indeed pacing back and forth through the hippies' backyard buck-ass naked.

Emotron had no body hair. He had shaved it all clean. The shaved body and the fact that Emotron was not particularly well endowed gave him the uncanny, uncomfortable, and unfortunate image of a naked, balding, little boy wearing thick old man glasses.

Not a pretty sight.

I feel the need to reaffirm for you at this point that this story is true. I am not using metaphor or hyperbole when I tell you what happened next: The naked Emotron picked up some sort of canister, sprayed his bald head, marched to the center of the yard, and set his head on fire.

The hippies barely stirred.

Emotron was not quite finished. For the final climatic gesture, he aimed the canister at his nether regions.

"No!" I thought.

"Yes!" The universe said.

Emotron set his baby boy penis ablaze.

The track came to a halt. Emotron bowed his recently flame-enveloped head low to the crowd, as though he suddenly cared about things like social convention, and the hippies politely clapped for him.

Emotron sauntered over to the side of the yard and started doing stretches and lunges. Still naked. But no one was paying attention to him anymore. They had moved on to other hippie activities.

I didn't understand. Did these people see what I had just seen?

I walked over to Emotron and said, "Wow, that was pretty amazing."

He looked at me and smiled. "Oh, thanks man."

We conversed for a short bit, and he actually seemed like a totally normal guy, outside of the curious hairdo and the fact that he was stark nude.

So how does something like the Emotron concert happen?

Less than a hundred years passed between the debut of "The Rite of Spring" and the debut of Emotron's flaming nether-regions. At "The Rite of Spring," the audience rioted because the chords were too dissonant. At the Emotron concert, people politely clapped and moved on.

We. Are. Numb.

Okay, most people in our society would probably have a stronger reaction to seeing Emotron than the hippies did. But the fact is, it takes a lot to get people's attention these days. LMFAO knows this. Lady Gaga knows this. Hollywood knows this. Emotron knows this.

The danger of art created to rise above the noise is that it may end up being noise itself.

Listening
In a quiet room with a friend, your speaking voice will most likely remain at a relatively low volume. In a crowded room, you may find yourself speaking at a slightly louder volume. In a war zone, you may find yourself

screaming into your friend's ear.

The noise around us determines how we speak. And how we listen.

Just as a conversation suffers in a war zone, art suffers in a culture built on noise. So does our enjoyment of it.

When is the last time you wept while listening to music?

Part of what it means to be fully alive is to fully experience the beauty of existence. That includes experiencing a full range of emotions in response to the sights, sounds, smells, and tastes of this good world.

How could a full human life consist of anything less than a robust, sensual experience of the goodness of creation? To be human is to be aware. Without awareness, which depends on our senses, we would be ignorant of existing at all. If we could not see, hear, touch, smell or taste, how would we know that we were alive? A sensual awareness is the conduit between ourselves and the goodness and beauty of the world around us.

Taste and see, sings the Psalmist.

Every one of our senses is potent enough to wash the mind in wonder of the extravagant goodness of the universe. Take Helen Keller, who was blind, deaf, and mute. Through the lone sense of touch that she possessed, she found a way to be connected to the world—to experience the full range of human emotion, communicate with others, and enjoy her life. In fact, she was able to do so more effectively than many others because in her extreme focus of touch, she developed a keen sense of awareness of her world. Without eyesight, she *saw* more clearly than many other people do with full eyesight.

Most of us today walk around with all five senses in fine working order, yet we lack the focus that allows us to truly taste and see. Our primary experience is limited to quick and shallow sensations and perceptions.

Like the story of the blind man whose eyes began to open at the command of Jesus, we *see men, but they look like trees.*

One atom is capable of producing an atomic explosion that can unleash unfathomable destruction. What if this nearly infinite potential exists in everything?

Maybe this explains the full emotional potential of music. Perhaps a single note truly and completely heard would overwhelm us as completely as staring directly at the noonday sun. Vibrations of sound with origins in the voice of the Creator himself, entering our consciousness through processes of intricate complexity . . . the crafting of instruments, perfecting of skills, vibrating air and eardrum, nerves and synapses and understanding, and *my God, it is all so magnificent!*

The single atom in the atomic bomb can lay waste to a city. Maybe one note of music holds within it the power to end war.

But we don't really listen. We may hear the note "C," but we hear it as a shadow of its truest form. Living, vibrant music devolves into dull noise, like the softening and blurring of the once-sharp and clear lines in the facial features of a long-lost love.

As a creator, are you ordering creation from a place of noise or a place of listening?

In my first jazz guitar lesson at the University of North Texas, my professor asked me to play a G major scale for him. I laughed and shredded out a G-major scale.

There you go. Next?

He paused and looked at me. He repeated himself:

"Could you please play a G-major scale for me?"

Confused, I spewed out another G-major scale. It was fast and sloppy, but I just wanted to move on to something else. I knew my G-major scale . . . I knew my G-major scale when I was twelve-years-old. This was college. I wanted to talk about melodic minor modes or alternate tunings or something more interesting than a G-major scale.

Once again, he paused.

"Do you think that sounds good?"

"Well, no, I guess not. Sorry."

I slowed down and played it cleaner.

"Ok, that's getting closer. Michael, you need to remember—this is music we are playing. Not scales."

That was perhaps one of the most important things I learned in college.

Our first several lessons, we didn't focus on learning how to play faster. He didn't teach me any exotic new scales or difficult pieces. We filed the edges off of my pick so that my tone would be smoother. We focused on playing really slow, really clean major scales. We focused on *listening*.

The person who creates from the noise simply adds to the noise. The person who creates from a place of listening, however, can actually make something worthwhile and enjoy his work in the process. Think of a writer who is still in love with words, or a cellist who is still inspired by the sound of bow across string.

Like an old married couple that needs to remind themselves of why they fell in love, ask yourself what it is about your craft that made you fall in love with it. Why do you do what you do and make what you make?

When the creator is submerged in the noise, she will have trouble attending properly to her work. Untended, gardens grow weeds. Passionate work devolves into mindless rote and heartless repetition. Dreams calcify into bread and butter.

I've found that when the joy has seeped out of the work, it is probably time to take a step back. My guitar professor had recognized that I had stopped listening. So he had me step back from modes and sweep picking to simple and slow major scales. In doing that, I was able to start rediscovering why I played guitar in the first place.

When I first started playing guitar, it was all so magical, like the early days of a dating relationship when all of the stories are heard for the first time. Every new chord was a new treasure. Before high school, most of my musical experience was in the "woodshed" (the practice room). I spent a lot of time by myself just trying to learn my craft. I loved playing the guitar. I loved the sound of the steel strings resonating through the cedar body. I loved how my own mind and body acclimated itself to the guitar as though it was becoming part of me. The fingertips of my left hand no longer blistered; the scales and strumming patterns that were so difficult months before were now second nature.

But at a certain point, some of the romance of playing the guitar turned into the romance of being a musician. Once I got to high school, I began playing for other people. This gave me a new social standing. I wasn't just the nerd with the thick glasses anymore. I was the nerd with thick glasses who played guitar. I started spending as much time on stage as I did in the practice room, and the experience of making music began to change. I was starting to build a reputation as a musician. There was a sort of ego gratification and social influence that the stage was starting to bring to my music.

One evening, I was playing at my church, and my dad was in the audience. He was watching me carefully as dads tend to do. At one point in the song, the bass player made a big mistake, and I shot him a quick vitriolic look.

He looked down, embarrassed, and kept playing. My dad noticed, and he asked me about it afterwards. I didn't think it was any big deal, and I kind of brushed it off. So my dad, who likes to make his points clearly, grounded me from my guitar for a month.

A month?!

My guitar was my life. I would have rather been grounded from food for a month. I was outraged.

But looking back, I see the wisdom of my dad's decision. I needed to back away from the guitar to learn how to love it properly again. In that month of musical celibacy, I actually became a better musician. My dad saw that I was starting to make my art about something else. It was starting to become about a stage. About ego and perfection. I was losing the joy of wood and steel beneath my fingers, losing the thrill of just playing music with my friends. He knew I needed to take a step back from all of it in order to see it. It was very Mr. Miyagi of him.

Creator, if what you are creating has grown insipid and dull, perhaps you ought to take a step back for a moment. Before you go back to your instrument, your pen, your brush—take a breath and remember how to listen again.

You cannot hear the fullness of the beauty in Rachmaninoff if you cannot hear the beauty in a single note.

Our art and our lives can be so much richer when we learn to really listen. To be fully human is to be fully engaged within the world—tasting, hearing, touching, seeing, and creating.

So back to Double Rainbow Guy…

Tens of millions of people watch his viral YouTube video and laugh at the absurdity of a (supposedly sober) grown man weeping and screaming in orgasmic pleasure over something as simple as moisture playing with light in the sky. But all of this makes me wonder if we should be laughing *with* Double Rainbow Guy rather than *at* him. Most of us watch him with the assumption that our jaded indifference to the colors of the rainbow is the norm, and that he is the less-than-sane one. But maybe he saw something that day that you and I haven't yet seen in a rainbow. Maybe he feels something that all of us would feel if we learned how to really see.

5. TECHNOLOGY : WOLFJAWS PHILOSOPHY

For a conservative Protestant Christian family in rural Wisconsin, the Gungors have produced an eclectic cast of characters.

I am the eldest of four, and by now you may have gathered that I am sort of odd. For those who may need further clarification, here is a picture of me moving out of my apartment a few years ago. Nothing about this photo was contrived—my wife just saw the state of things and thought it was worth a photograph.

My siblings are no more normal than I am.

Rob is the second oldest. If you want to see a picture of Rob, you can go to iamthecoolestmanalive.com. Rob works in San Francisco designing websites, but he is starting to focus his energy on his new expression of blues music under the artist name "Wolfjaw." Rob has a medicinal license for a certain type of herb that he enjoys partaking of, although the argument for its medical necessity to his health is dubious at best. Rob normally has long hair and a long beard, and he wears a crystal around his neck. He recently shaved his beard, though, and I told him it left him with the look of a soprano sax player.

I was surprised to find myself in a conversation recently with Rob about the "anointing."

For those who didn't grow up in the kinds of religious circles that I did, I should explain. The anointing is something that people in charismatic churches talked a lot about in the 90s. We sang songs about it and asked that it would "fall on us." The anointing is not something that I would expect a ganja-loving blues singer who calls himself Wolfjaw to talk about very much.

But we're hanging out, and out of nowhere, Rob is explaining to me how he had felt the anointing at the Güngör concert he had attended when we were in San Francisco: "It's like all of this positive electricity firing in your brain and then when you extend that energy into the room with the strumming of a guitar or by singing, and even more so when you amplify it through a sound system, that energy only gets magnified and it just sends all that anointing into the room. You know?"

I smile and nod, hoping that he will continue this line of thought. He does: "It's kind of like the opposite of a haunting. When something horrible happens, that energy or spirit just stays there, but the anointing is the opposite of that."

As far as I know, Rob is not a person who would call himself a Christian at this point. And he is certainly not the type of Christian that you would expect to have a conversation with about the anointing. For me, hearing Rob talk about the anointing was like listening to a nun cuss a blue streak.

Rob continued. "This is why I don't use Pro Tools anymore. When you cut up the performance like everybody is doing today into all of these bits and pieces, you lose the anointing. You lose the energy of that moment when you chop it up like that, taking one moment from here and one from there . . . "

I am laughing, enjoying every word of this peculiar soapbox. But I do feel the need to interject the observation that with a crystal dangling beneath his long beard, Rob looks like some sort of sage. He smiles but plows ahead.

"Also, in Pro Tools, you are turning music into ones and zeroes. You lose the anointing with that as well. When you record to analog tape, it's actually physical grooves that you are creating. There is a natural degradation in the energy—it's not this simulated, digital shit that totally loses the anointing."

I had to admit that Wolfjaw was making some interesting points.

For one, technology has absolutely changed the way we think, live, and create art.

Photoshop allows the amateur photographer to create a visual representation of nearly anything she can imagine. A person with lousy pitch can auto-tune his voice to sound more pitch-perfect than Pavarotti. A composer doesn't need to know how to transpose the trumpet part because the notation program does it for him. It's a different world for artists than it ever has been.

Technology has always influenced and given birth to new forms of art, but for the first time in history, technology is moving faster than any of us are able to keep up with. The benefits of all of this technology are vast, and the creative opportunities that it can potentially open up for artists are limitless.

Because of Internet, for instance, the musician doesn't *need* a label anymore to get his music "out there." The poet in rural Mississippi isn't limited to her small community. An entire world is available to her through her computer—communities of artists with whom she can share and learn from are only a few clicks away.

Because of technological advances, you don't have to have a million dollars to record a great-sounding record. You can download free recording software to use as you write and record. Everyday people have inexpensive technology at their fingertips to create a short film, write and self-publish a novel, or dabble in graphic design. All of this means greater accessibility and opportunity—the growing democratization of art. Everyone has a shot, and the sky is the limit.

As amazing as all of this opportunity is, though, there are some pitfalls to all of this luxury and technological convenience. For starters, there is the danger of Grey Goo.

In the documentary *PressPausePlay* (2011), Moby mentions the danger of art becoming like Grey Goo in our society. Grey Goo is a popular end-of-the-world scenario that has been used in sci-fi novels and video games. The phrase refers to the idea of a self-replicating nanobot that would consume everything organic while replicating itself, leaving the entire world in an amorphous blob of grey goo.

So here's the idea as it relates to art—what would happen to the book industry if every person on earth wrote and published a book? How would you even start to find the good books? The democratization of art carries the danger of the masses burying the most talented among us in sheer volume.

"Eventually, the world is just covered with mediocrity," Moby says. "And people start to get comfortable with mediocrity."

John-ness

Another danger of technology is that it lessens the demand for human craft. Rob referred to a program called Pro Tools, one of the more popular pieces of recording software. What a lot of music listeners may not understand today is that a person who uses these programs to record doesn't have to be very talented to sound good. A singer with awful pitch can auto-tune herself. A drummer doesn't have to play in time to sound like he has "pocket"; he just has to know how to push "quantize" in the plug-in, and the computer will automatically shift every note into perfect time for him. This is the "chopping up" that my brother was railing against.

When we listen to most current pop music, we are in essence hearing computers spitting out ones and zeroes. The sound may have begun with a human voice or musician, just as a computer animation may start with a photograph of a human figure. But the end result is computer generated. Most popular music today is more mechanical and less human than it has ever been, and I think Wolfjaw is right—we lose something important when we lose the humanness within the music.

There's this pianist named John who plays in my band sometimes. He doesn't do much in life other than play and practice piano, so he's quite a formidable pianist but also socially eccentric.

Quick John story for you.

One time after a gig, our band decided to go eat at the Cheesecake Factory. We were all acting a little rowdy as the adrenaline from the night was still wearing off. On the way into the restaurant from the parking lot, one of the band guys ran up behind John and "pantsed" him. John was wearing baggy athletic shorts, and when they were pulled down, everything else underneath was pulled down with them.

Most people would blush and quickly pull up their pants. Not John. John looked at all of us with bewilderment, and then made a gesture with his arms as if to say, "Seriously? You want to see this? Fine with me." The pants stayed down.

After a few seconds, our laughter began to fade. Horror dawned as we realized that those pants were staying down. The laughter gave way to pleading.

"John! What are you doing? Pull your pants up! Are you crazy?!"

John turned the situation around, making us the ones who were embarrassed to be standing with the naked guy in the Cheesecake Factory parking lot. After he had tormented us long enough, he finally pulled up his pants, and we walked in to the restaurant, knowing full well whom the victor was in the situation. Bold move by John. But also kind of brilliant, because to my knowledge, no one in the band has ever tried to do anything like that to him again.

There's something about John that is utterly and only John, and that also comes through his music. John plays the piano in a way that can take control of a room. He uses notes at least as efficiently as dropped shorts to communicate what he needs to communicate. John has spent enough time in the practice room to develop a high level of precision and virtuosity in his playing. Some elements of his craft can be emulated with MIDI programming and quantization. What cannot be emulated is the essence of John's humanity that comes through his playing. When John strikes a piano key, his well-trained hands aren't simply engaging in mathematical precision. His hands carry stories, emotions, doubts, and passions, all unique to John. A man cannot spend thousands of hours sitting at a piano without having some of his soul soak into the wood.

Virtuosity is not simply about playing quickly or accurately. The virtuoso is someone who has developed his skill to the point where his tools and instruments become like an organic extension of himself.

It's like when a person masters a language—she doesn't have to think about the words as much as the ideas that she would like to communicate. For the fluent, the words don't get in the way. This is virtuosity. When the bow and neck of the violin becomes part of the violinist's body, when the programming language becomes as natural as the native language, when the brush of the painter moves with ease and precision—that is when the artist can truly create unshackled.

Virtuosity allows the human soul to print itself more clearly onto the canvas, blueprint, improvisation, or composition.

As sophisticated as Pro Tools may get in cleaning up the technicalities of a performance, it will never be able to imprint the human spirit onto a grid. A professor of mine once suggested that people would soon start attending concerts where the music would be both composed and performed by computers. His argument was that there are computers now that can compose new pieces of music that are every bit as technically brilliant and mathematically beautifully as Mozart or Bach.

What my nerdy professor (who probably spent way too much time with MIDI sax controllers) didn't understand was that the vast majority of people don't listen to music for the mathematics of its theory or the precision of its execution. Music is human. It speaks of hearts and pain. To a mother, the cry of a baby is more than frequencies and velocities. To a new fiancé, an engagement ring is more than smelted rock. Music is one human soul speaking to another. It is emotion and experience translated into ivory and ebony, nylon and stretched animal skin. Even when coded into ones and zeroes, the intent of good music is never to simply create mathematical formulas, but to communicate the human soul.

Technology as a Crutch
One of the practical results of our reliance on technology in music is that it disconnects the tangible and measurable results of virtuosity from good old-fashioned hard work. As long as someone can get close to the correct notes and rhythms, the technology can easily take him the rest of the way. On a purely technical level, sure, technology can make up for human error. On a human and unquantifiable level—the level of the soul—much is lost when we fill every pore and wrinkle with plastic "perfection."

In 2008, a controversy erupted over a man named Oscar Pistorius. Oscar wanted to compete in the Olympics, but he had prosthetic lower legs. He was disqualified at first because many people believed that his advanced carbon-fiber feet would give him an advantage over people with plain old human legs and feet. That decision was eventually reversed. Pistorius did not qualify for the South African team in 2008, but he did in 2012.

Imagine if Oscar Pistorius had beaten everyone at the Olympics by a landslide. Then imagine if in the next Olympics, you saw three or four people with even more advanced cybernetic limbs that could be used even by people with healthy limbs, making them so fast that no normal human being could compete. Then imagine fifty years from now, when every athlete is relying on cybernetics. What would happen to the athleticism of Olympians? Why would someone spend all of his energy training when someone else can design a faster limb and leave him in the dust?

What happens to musicians when we don't have to learn to play in time with other musicians because all we have to do is push the quantize button? The musical result in our culture so far is that we are listening to the most in-time, in-tune music in the history of the world made by some of the least practiced, least developed musicians.

I don't think technology is inherently destructive to art. On the contrary, I think it opens up all sorts of new possibilities. Artists ought to use and explore technology and all of the potential that it opens up creatively, but we also ought to be guarded against using that technology as a crutch for our own artistic shortcomings.

For the creator, technology will make a much better servant than a master.

6. FIRST WORLD MINDSET: THE DECLINE OF THE U.S. EMPIRE

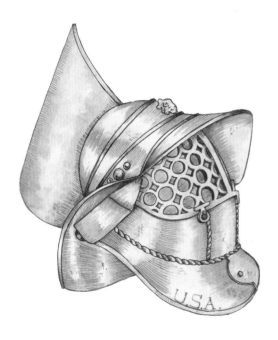

Indolence has destroyed the arts.
--Pliny, ancient Roman author

After ancient Rome conquered all the people that they wanted to conquer and fought all the battles that needed to be fought, after they had become the most powerful empire in the world, it all began to crumble beneath them. They had what they wanted, and they started to get bored.

In cultures like these, entertainment often becomes paramount. When a culture's greatest enemy is boredom, its greatest savior is entertainment. Rome's answer to this problem was the coliseum. Vicious gladiators fought each other to a bloody, gruesome death in front of a roaring crowd. Slaves and prisoners would be thrown into the arena to be torn apart by wild animals as the Romans laughed and drank. They would sometimes fill the arena with water and stage huge naval battles, killing hundreds or thousands, until the water was thick and red with blood.

The empire that had everything it ever wanted turned its bored eyes to entertainment to keep the adrenaline flowing. It also turned to sex. Prostitution was common, and it was also acceptable for older men to have sex with teenage boys and girls, as long as the men stayed in the "masculine" role sexually.

After hundreds of years of uncontested world power, Rome spiraled into brutal violence, sexual perversion, and dehumanizing exhibitionism—all for the sake of entertainment.

Idiocracy

America is no longer the empire that it once was. We've fallen behind in education, health care, and other crucial areas. And what about our entertainment? What about our art?

Certainly, a lot of great art is being made in the U.S. today, but it is generally relegated to the sidelines. As I've said, our most popular art is that which can elicit the fastest visceral response in the consumer, which means that more and more art is aiming at our basest instincts.

Several years ago, the movie *Idiocracy* addressed the devolution of American society. A normal shlub of a guy from the early twenty-first century visits the future, and he finds that humans have become complete idiots. The people of the future barely know how to communicate in full sentences. They water their plants with Gatorade because marketers told them that the plants need the electrolytes. Everything in the culture of the future revolves around entertainment and sex—Starbucks is still in existence, for example, but now people can order various sexual favors at the drive-thru along with their coffee.

Is our culture headed toward *Idiocracy*?

If our culture-makers have to keep stooping lower in order to burrow beneath the audience's boredom, where will it end?

How much farther can shock comedies go to keep our attention? In 1987, audiences who went to see *Planes, Trains, and Automobiles* were shocked to laughter by the idea of John Candy's hand being in between Steve Martin's butt cheeks while they slept. The camera didn't even show us Candy's hand sandwiched between Martin's cheeks—the film just made the suggestion, and it worked. In 2010s *Due Date*, (which is kind of like a present-day *Planes, Trains, and Automobiles*) the awkward sexual tension between the two traveling partners is ratcheted up a few levels. This time, we see the face and hear the very awkward sounds of a masturbating Zach Galifianakis in the passenger seat while Robert Downey Jr. tries to sleep in the seat next to him. This blockbuster comedy scene makes the moment between Steve Martin and John Candy in the earlier movie look like an innocuous scene from of a Disney movie.

Even for movies only a couple of years apart, like *The Hangover* (2009) and *The Hangover 2* (2011), the filmmakers feel they have to top themselves in how far they will go. In the first film, we were shocked to laughter by the fact that Stu had married a prostitute in his drug-induced Las Vegas adventure. In the second film, Stu has sex with a partial transvestite prostitute in Thailand. He/she has both breasts and male genitals, and both are displayed in full glory on the big screen.

What will it take for comedies a decade or two from now to shock us? How can violence stay shocking and scary as we get more and more bored with the special effects and violence that we see every day? Where does it end? When the violence is actually real? When we make a reality show equivalent of the Roman Coliseum?

This may sound exaggerated to our sensible modern ears, but stranger things have happened in history.

America has lately been in the "Jackass" and "Keeping Up with the Kardashians" stage of our decline. Reality TV, pop music, violent video games and porn are our culture's prescriptions against boredom. If we're not so bad as Rome, then maybe we're only in the earlier stages of our decline.

Regardless of what the end result is, these are the fruits of our cultural tree.

Remember, ancient Rome once thrived with art. The Romans did with sculpture, murals, portraits, and architecture things that no other culture in the world had ever done. They borrowed from and expanded upon the artistic endeavors of previous great empires, and their work has been passed down through history.

But as the Roman Empire began its decline, its art began to change. Rome became lazy. Historians tell us that the Roman calendar had over 180 holidays and festivals. After the wars had been won and the arena games had taken over the culture, Rome began to express its comfort with sloppier art. The sharp, ornate carvings of stone that was characteristic of earlier days devolved into more abstract shapes. The passion and precision of their art faded with the fading passion and pain of their wars. Laziness, comfort, entitlement, boredom—these have never been the great motivations for the pinnacles of human creativity. Not in ancient Rome, not in present-day North America.

I recognize that many—too many—Americans struggle materially, but by and large, our present culture is a society of people enjoying the fruits of the steadfast struggling and victories of the people who have gone before us. The rest of us haven't had to do much struggling, especially relative to the struggles of generations past. We've become accustomed to blessing. We take things like food and clean water for granted, and feel that a strong cell phone service signal is an inalienable human right. America has had it quite easy for a while.

Our main problems are what one popular blog has labeled "first world problems." These are problems like: "We sat on the tarmac with the AC off and no Wi-Fi for twenty minutes after boarding the plane." Or: "I had to spit out my ice cube because it wasn't made with filtered water." "Daylight Savings Time has completely thrown off my TV viewing schedule." "It's nap time and my housekeeper is not done cleaning. How will I sleep?"

Have you ever had a homeless person reject the leftovers you offered him because he wasn't a fan of that particular restaurant's club sandwiches? Only someone who is homeless in the first world would be so picky.

I was talking to an American girl who was working at an orphanage in Africa, and she was telling me about how her perspective of poverty has changed. When she came back to the States and saw the people asking her for money on the street corner, she'd look down at their Nike shoes, and think, "You have shoes. You are not poor." She told me that she makes a lot less money working at the orphanage than the average American street panhandler does, and she was probably right.

When you don't have to deal with things like losing most of your friends and family to famine or genocide, when you don't have to deal with things like losing your parents to HIV or not having clean water to give your starving children, it is easy to start thinking that not having a date this weekend is the end of the world. We start thinking that the sluggishness of our five-year-old computer is a problem beyond the scope of human ability to cope.

What's both funny and sad about first world problems is that we really do suffer over them. My daughter, Amélie, really does suffer when we don't let her eat the entire chocolate cake. She responds as though everything good in the world has suddenly ceased to exist and she is left to die on the banks of the River Styx.

I am very thankful to be in a country where we don't have suffer as many of the dreadful injustices that so many others have suffered in other times and places. But if we don't stay mindful of how good we really have it, remaining grateful and vigilant against entitlement, it is easy to become victims to spoiled silliness.

Many in our society have become like Veruca Salt in Willie Wonka's chocolate factory: "I want a feast! I want a bean feast! Cream buns and doughnuts and fruitcake with no nuts so good you could go nuts . . . I want a ball! I want a party, pink macaroons and a million balloons and performing baboons and give it to me NOW!"

Like the Romans, we turn to entertainment to save us from our purposeless boredom. So the filmmakers try to keep up. *The Hangover* only shocks once. *The Hangover 2* only shocks once. They have to keep digging lower and lower to stay beneath our boredom. The music industry tries to keep up. They make songs more explicit, sexier, shorter, more compressed and auto-tuned. Modern art expresses our boredom with nihilistic sloppiness and shocking displays of violence or sexuality.

Certainly, lewd and bawdy art has been around for a long time. Shakespeare plays have their share of shocking scenes, but they have complexity and profundity, too.

When art becomes a mere distraction from our first-world boredom, it will devolve into something less human. It will become animalistic and trite. But it will certainly be entertaining.

Part of the reason people aren't building cathedrals anymore is that we are too lazy and spoiled for the pain and the work that they demand from us. This sort of laziness leads to an artistic narcissism that creates art as a mere emotional expression of the ego rather than an intentional and profound re-ordering or re-imagining of the world. Art schools and galleries start filling up with self-indulgent narcissists who think that every fart of theirs is a work of genius because "it came from *deep inside of me.*"

Entitlement is not a friend of art. Work is. Pain is.

Pain is that blessed and despised universal experience that creates more true art than any other human experience. Love is racked with pain. Life's most joyful experiences—the birth of a newborn baby, the formation of deep friendship, or first consummation of love—all are associated with an experience of pain. A wedding is the joyful union of two lovers, but it begins with, "Who gives this bride away?"

Pain is as common as skin. We enter this world in pain, struggling for our first breath, and when we leave, we struggle for our last. Life ends when that struggle ends. So does good art.

Pain is not the same thing as suffering. One can fully experience the pain of life without being the tortured artist who lives in constant agony. But creation is no easy task. Good art demands a fight.

7. CAPITALISM: PAYING THE PEAR-SHAPED SUPERMAN

Imagine that you are walking down a street in your neighborhood, just enjoying your day, when a sudden movement in the corner of your peripheral vision catches your attention. You glance over and see a little girl running full speed toward the street, chasing a ball. You scan the street for traffic, and sure enough, a car is quickly approaching, closing in. The little girl doesn't see it. The driver doesn't see the girl. You call to the girl, wave your arms, but she's lost in play.

The car is about to plow into the girl, and there's nothing you can do about it. You run toward the site of the inevitable crash, preparing for the worst. Then you see him. Someone is running toward the girl from a different direction. And he just might make it. You squint your eyes—he's got dark curls, a booty that's unusually large in relation to the rest of his body. Is that . . .? It is! It's Michael Gungor!

Certainly he is too far away to reach her in time . . . but like an ever-so-slightly pear-shaped Superman, he is running at an uncanny speed toward the imperiled youngster. Just as the girl is about to step into the street and meet her untimely demise, Gungor swoops in with superhuman speed and seizes her into his arms. The car hurtles by. The child is saved.

You exhale. A woman runs toward the rescued child: "Oh my God! Baby, are you okay? Oh my goodness, thank you sir! Thank you so much!"

Gungor wipes a bead of sweat off of his substantial brow, which his mother long ago assured him was just the right size to accommodate his big brain. He says to the woman, nonchalantly, "Of course. I'm just glad I saw her there."

"Oh, wow, my heart is beating so fast," says the woman. "Seriously, thank you so much. Is there anything I can do for you? You saved my daughter's life!"

You look at Michael as he gives the woman a warm smile. He shakes his head. "No ma'am, I don't need you to do anything for me. It was my pleasure . . .

"But you know what? Actually, since you asked, why don't you just go ahead and write me a check for, like, 300 bucks."

The woman pauses. "Oh, okay. Really?"

"Yeah, yeah, it's no big deal. But you know, I did save your daughter's life and all. I think she's worth far more than a few hundred bucks, don't you? I mean, it really was my pleasure to do it, but . . . yeah, Gungor is spelled G-U-N . . ."

End of scenario.

Money may be the primary standard of value in our culture, but it also has an uncanny ability to cheapen things.

Children of Capitalism

One of Karl Marx's arguments against capitalism was that it has the tendency to take over every aspect of society. In *The Communist Manifesto*, he wrote, "The need of a constantly expanding market for its products chases the bourgeoisie over the whole surface of the globe. It must nestle everywhere, settle everywhere, establish connections everywhere." It is the nature of market economies to render everything a commodity.

Touring with a band involves a lot of "hurry up and wait" time, a lot of sitting in passenger vans and green rooms. One of the things our band does to pass the time in these situations is to play "How Much Would it Cost?" The game is simple. We simply ask one another how much it would cost to do things that are less than preferable. The scenarios are always ridiculous—like, "How much would it cost for you to have your nipples transplanted to your neck?" Or, "How much would it cost for you to send a picture of your naked butt to every person in your contact list without an apology or explanation?"

About an hour ago, we were sitting in the Houston airport and having this conversation: "If someone paid you a thousand dollars a day to live in this airport, and you could never go outside, how long would you stay?"

The cellist answered "six months." The guitarist answered "ten years," but then thought more about it and changed it to five years instead.

We are children of capitalism. We live in a society that puts a price tag on everything that we can think of.

There are prisons in some cities that now offer a cleaner, more private prison-cell upgrade for $90 a night.

The Subway sandwich corporation, despite the fact that they did not come up with the idea of calling something that is twelve inches in length a "footlong," has attempted to trademark the word "footlong" so that anyone else that would like to use the common phrase would have to pay Subway for the rights. In response, a clever NPR reporter commented on the story, "We don't know yet if mass transit systems will be suing Subway for its use of the term 'subway.'"

In Utah, a woman was paid $10,000 by an online casino to permanently tattoo her forehead with their web address.

There are websites that sell the stars of our galaxy, posting banner ads like: "Buy a Star from $19.95."

In Europe, you can pay a little over ten dollars for the right to emit one metric ton of carbon dioxide into the atmosphere. It seems to me that ten bucks is a pretty good bargain for the right to pollute our planet.

Should everything in the universe really have a price tag on it?

Putting Price Tags on Art

When art becomes a mere commodity to be traded like a sack of potatoes or bushel of corn, it is cheapened.

Capitalism tends to do to art what value meals do to cuisine. Think of what the food industry in our nation has done to our food. When dollars and cents are the sole purpose for the manufacturing and distribution of food, the food suffers. We suffer. The mass production, hormones and pesticides that have allowed the food industry to make more money have made our food less nutritious than it ever has been. Animals are treated cruelly. People get fat and sick and die.

When money is the primary value for art, the primary indicator for the quality of the work is how much it can sell, and the natural course of the artist will be to aim for the masses, to produce the work as cheaply and easily as possible. The work suffers. It is less nourishing. Art as industry prods artists to think in terms of marketing channels rather than more substantive building blocks of art like beauty, emotion, protest, or honesty. Seth Godin comments about the nature of art as industry:

> Art has been around for a really long time. Music has been around for a really long time. Painting and sculpture and plays have been around for a really long time. But it's only in the last fifty years that there's been an industry . . . they call it the music industry, the movie industry . . . that's new . . . . It used to be, you didn't become an artist to become rich, you became an artist because you had an idea to share, cause you had an emotion to share[1].

Of course, artists have made a living with their art for a lot longer than fifty years, and it's not as though all artists of yesteryear had pure intentions, but Godin makes an interesting point. Being an artist is different in an era where art is big business. Creative endeavors like filmmaking, video game production, publishing, music, and design are multi-billion dollar industries. Actors are no longer confined to the lifestyles of lowly court jesters or traveling Elizabethan acting troupes. Famous actors and musicians can become stars that are treated like gods on the earth. Successful architects, web designers, or novelists can become wealthy and powerful people.

It's easy to see how capitalism and industry can tarnish honest artistic expression, but many argue that the ridding the artistic world of marketplace considerations won't help us either.

Ayn Rand, a staunch supporter of capitalism, wrote her philosophies through the words of the characters of her novels. In *Atlas Shrugged*, a

---

1 From an interview in the documentary, *PressPausePlay* 2011

composer is venting to the protagonist about the state of art in the world. He says, "If there is more tragic a fool than the businessman who doesn't know that he's an exponent of man's highest creative spirit—it's the artist who thinks that the businessman is his enemy."

Rand's reasoning is that good business shares many of the same qualities as good art. They both involve ingenuity and creativity. They both engineer reality according to their metaphysical value judgments. As you'll recall from my earlier definitions of art, I agree with Rand on this point. I used to separate categories like business and art as polar opposites. But I now think that on some level, art and business share the same soil. The very act of an artist sharing his art with any other person becomes a sort of commercialization of that art—even if the transacted value is something more ambiguous and non-financial like joy or satisfaction. And this isn't necessarily a bad thing, because every human interaction involves a transaction of values.

To illustrate this, let's go back to the hero scenario posed at the beginning of this chapter. This time, I'll change the story slightly . . .

You are walking down the street in your neighborhood . . . *fast forward . . . you start running . . . fast forward . . .* Gungor swoops in . . . *fast forward . . .* the child is saved.

This time, the mother walks slowly out of the house towards Michael, who is bent over panting from his run. As the mother finally reaches him, he places the daughter's hand in the mother's, and says, "Here you go, ma'am."

In response, the mother ignores his presence entirely.

She looks at her daughter with indifference, mumbling, "Okay, let's go inside now."

You have reached us by now, and you're indignant. "Excuse me, Miss, did you not see what happened? This man saved your daughter's life. She almost got hit by that car!"

The woman peers at you, bored. "Yeah, so what?"

Wouldn't that make you wonder if this woman even loved her daughter? Isn't the appropriate response to thank this bubble-assed Latino? (With that kind of speed, he must have some extra muscles in that thing or something.)

You would probably feel a level of outrage in that situation because it lacked the proper transactions of human values. There was no mutual respect, no gratitude offered by the woman who owed it.

So what are the appropriate transacted values for the creation and enjoyment of art?

Every artist has an incentive for making art. No one dedicates his life to art for no reason. That incentive might be money. It might be recognition. A sense of accomplishment. The satisfaction of sharing beauty with others. These are all price tags that the artist hangs on his work.

Some price tags are more healthy and appropriate than others.

As a professional artist, I recognize that artists need money to live just as much as anyone else does in society. I also believe that a society does well to have artists that can spend all of their working energy on their art. Without a way for artists to make a living with their art, they have to get other jobs. This limits their ability to focus the majority of their energy on their art. I'm not sure about you, but I don't want my favorite artists to spend less energy and time on their work. That would take away from both the artist and the society that benefits from the artist's work.

Still, in a capitalistic society, the temptation is to equate the value of work with the dollars and cents that it earns.

Not every artist has to make a living making art. Millions of people who play guitar would do well to keep their day jobs. Plenty of people make incredible art "on the side." William Faulkner wasn't any less of an artist for writing *As I Lay Dying* on the back of a wheelbarrow during breaks in his job shoveling coal for the electric company. An artist is not someone who is paid for his art. An artist is someone who makes art. In a capitalistic society, it is especially important to remember this distinction.

It is also important to remember that some of the greatest artists in history weren't able to make a good living with their art during their lifetime. Henry David Thoreau, Herman Melville, and Emily Dickinson never received much recognition or money for their work during their lifetime. Van Gough's paintings sell for millions of dollars today, but in his lifetime, few people cared about his work. Sometimes brilliant artists are simply too far ahead of the curve. They are like Marty McFly in *Back to the Future*, explaining his outlandish rock-and-roll guitar solo to the puzzled faces of his peers: "Your kids are going to love it."

While it is unfortunate that some of the best artists in society will have to struggle financially, both the professional and the nonprofessional artist would do well to remember that art's primary value system shouldn't be monetary. Art is too soul-ish, like love or sex, to be treated like a mere commodity. The value of the art must be indicated by something more than how many people like it or how much money it earns. This can be particularly difficult for Americans, who so often find their identity in what they are paid to do.

Our culture is faced with the temptation to tie our sense of worth to our level of production in the world. This is as true for the artist as for anyone else. In a culture like ours, it is easy to believe that the measuring stick of value for our art is money or popularity. But chances are, some of the best art being made right now is invisible to you and me.

Great art is being programmed by the dad who retreats into his studio after putting the kids to bed. It is being penned by the schoolteacher during the short breaks in her day. Many great artists will never sign a record contract or be featured on radio or TV, but are creating extraordinary things. Our children and children's children will know who these people are, even if we don't.

In our society of consumption, so many people give their entire lives to the acquisition of wealth, often forgetting the importance of so many other values in the process. Bigger houses, nicer cars, more toys to play with—but what's the point if we are too burned out and numb from our greed to actually enjoy any of it?

And what do you benefit if you gain the whole world but lose your own soul? At the end of the day, capitalism is not the enemy of art when it stays in its proper place in the artistic endeavor. But capitalism has the tendency to make money the central and most important human value in our dealings with others. Money is too often the primary measuring stick that we use to judge the value of something, but there are other values that are healthier measuring sticks for determining the value of human work. Beauty. Truth. Honesty. The exploration of the human spirit. The expression of real love. Money is not the root of all kinds of evil. The love of money is. It's also the root of a lot of bad art.

Selling Out

Steve plays in a well-known Christian band, and he hates what he does. He gets on stage night after night, but believes that he is making the world a worse place by doing so. Friends of Steve often tell him that he needs to quit and do something else. He is smart and talented, but it's a comfortable and well-paying gig for him, and his fear keeps him locked into a lifeless status quo.

Steve is unhappy, cynical and jaded. In an attempt to escape his misery, he is becoming chemically dependent. He wasn't always this way. When

Steve is healthy, he is the life of the party. He can be brilliant, witty, and hilarious. But in recent years, he spends all of his artistic energy creating aesthetics that don't align with the values of his internal world because he gets paid well to do it. Consequently, his soul has taken quite a beating.

Why does he do it? Because there is a voice that tells him that he's not okay. This voice tells him that he needs to take the work to be safe. He needs some kind of external signs of security because he has none inside. So he builds his life around these worried voices inside his head.

This doesn't happen on a conscious level with most people. Most sellouts don't think they are selling their soul; they think they are just doing what is necessary. They aren't even aware of the lies that the fearful voices are whispering into their ears.

The reality is, if Steve didn't take that gig, he would not starve to death. He would be fine. But he doesn't see that. He just *feels* that he *needs* to do what he is doing.

Selling out is never worth it.

Selling your soul for money, recognition, or any otherworldly good is like selling your hearing for a music collection. It's pointless. What good is the music if you can't hear it? No amount of money or power is worth even a shred of the human soul.

Selling out is not always so cut and dry, though. It's not always for such obvious prizes as money or power. Sometimes it is masked in good intentions. Sometimes selling out feels like friendship or loyalty. It can masquerade in powerful words like obedience or honor. But when a person crafts their external world in a way that is not true to their internal world, even positive motivators like these are not enough. It still is a lie. It still is selling out; it just has a different reward—popularity, cred, being perceived as polite or classy, and so on.

How does the artist know if she is being honest or if she is selling out?

The very act of creation ought to connect the artist more deeply with the ground of his humanity. It ought to align with that inner Muse. When it doesn't, we create in a way that separates us from our true humanity—this is selling out.

We are depressed, but we craft our world to look like a big plastic smiley face.

We are hurt, but we bury our true feelings in mockery and cynicism.

The artist that lies with his aesthetic is in a dangerous place. When you craft your external world out of values that aren't true to your inner world, your inner world will soon begin to crumble. Eventually your outer world follows suit and begins to crumble as well.

I think this plays a part in why so many stars overdose on drugs and why so many preachers and politicians wind up in sex scandals. They have created outer worlds that their inner worlds can't sustain, like building a house on sand.

To create art, you need building materials. Not just physical materials like canvas, film, or banjos. First, you need an internal supply of building materials like vision, determination, and inspiration. Products of the soul. You can feel these kinds of materials being manufactured by your soul when your heart is moved by a great film or your mind is opened in a profound conversation with a friend. When you leave the noise behind to go spend a few hours in the mountains or just have a good hearty laugh. Those moments are like fires of the soul, churning out material that the artist can access in the creation of her work.

However, dishonest art cannot draw from these things. The materials won't cooperate. They just won't bend in the right places or fit into the right slots.

None of us can create *ex nihilo*, and dishonest art, like honest art, has to come from somewhere. When artists lie with their aesthetic, it becomes as if they are borrowing creative material from the very substance of their soul. When the outer work demands payment, and the soul has nothing that it can use to pay the debt, it offers a tiny piece of itself.

This is the essence of selling out, and it's never worth it. Regardless of the intention, the result is still the same: the quieting of the soul, the quieting of the internal Voice.

8. CELEBRITY: SIGN THESE PYTHONS

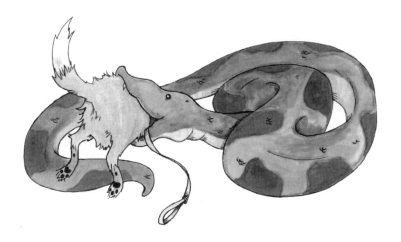

Spirits were high at Marshfield Christian School when news came that "Toymaker's Dream" was coming to town again. The air was abuzz in anticipation of the most exhilarating dance production any of us had ever seen. Marshfield didn't tend to make the tour city list on the back of U2 shirts. But it did for "Toymaker's Dream." The production had come to our church several times throughout my childhood, and I knew most of the songs by heart. The fact that I had seen it several times already didn't curb my excitement in the least.

An entirely different cast was performing "Toymaker" now, and I could not wait to see if there would be any new twists. They used pyrotechnics and laser lights last time. A fifth grader in central Wisconsin in the 90s couldn't hope for much more.

One of my favorite characters was played by a large black man with a mohawk who wore black leather football shoulder pads with spikes coming out of them. After I saw him the first time, my sole purpose in life was to purchase some football shoulder pads so I could pretend I was him. My brothers and I would re-enact a doo-wop song from "Toymaker" where he parades around the stage, flinging girls over his arms and flexing his enormous biceps for the audience's *oohs* and *ahs*. My fifth grade arms were girlish and hairless—kind of like they are now—and I couldn't believe how big and manly this guy's biceps were. Each one looked like a python that had swallowed a couple of small dogs.

One of the dancers was slated to stay at our house that year, and I was giddy with nervous excitement. A *famous* person was going to be staying at *my* house. In reality, this girl was actually a volunteer intern who had raised money to go on the road with this Christian ministry. To everyone else on the planet, neither she nor her production was famous. But I felt like Madonna was spending the night at our house.

I remember competing with all of the other kids after the production to see who could get the most autographs from the dancers.

"Look, I got Jesus to sign my poster!"

"Oh yeah? Well, I got the devil to sign my arm!"

That was a pretty big deal. If you got the devil to sign your arm, you wouldn't be bathing for a while.

Fast-forward a few years . . .

I was fourteen and visiting some friends in Minnesota. Some family friends had invited me to their church's youth group. I was reluctant because, like I've said, I was a pretty shy person, and I didn't have much interest in trying to meet a bunch of new people in a new city. I didn't want to be rude, though, so I went.

I felt awkward as I walked into the sterile grey youth room. Nobody said anything to me, and I wasn't the kind of kid who was going to strike up some small talk about the weather or whatever extroverted strangers enjoy talking to one another about. I noticed that I was getting a few curious stares, which I interpreted as "Who is this weirdo?" My strategy was to blend in to the grey of the walls and chairs. I saw an empty row that would be a safe place to sit without upsetting any sort of tribal rules or hierarchies.

I sat in my seat, waiting anxiously for the service to start so I wouldn't look like such a loser. Before long, my waiting was interrupted by a group of cool kids who seemed to want to sit together in my otherwise empty row. There were some cute girls in the group, and I hoped one of them would sit next to me rather than the douche-y looking guys they were with.

As they started making their way into the row, I noticed a sort of jostling and stutter of movement. One of the girls said to her friend, "You sit there," pointing at the seat next to me.

The friend seemed to think that this was the damnation of unthinkable atrocity. She blurted, either not realizing or caring that I could hear her, "I'm not sitting next to him. *You* sit next to him!"

My cheeks warmed and my shoulders lifted ever so slightly towards my ears—perhaps in instinctual homage to some prehistoric gesture learned to protect our brains from harm. I looked around, trying to pretend like I hadn't heard. The service started soon enough, but all I wanted was to get out of there as quickly as possible. But then something happened.

The youth pastor recognized me. He had seen me play a guitar solo at a youth conference that our church had put on the year before. Either he had been impressed or was trying to burn through some time, but he introduced me to the whole youth group with accolades and asked if I could come up to the stage and play for everybody. After some goading, I reluctantly consented.

After I played, things felt different in that cold, grey room. When the service ended, I encountered the warmth of smiling eyes and friendly introductions rather than the curious and skeptical glances that I had experienced before the service. Suddenly, the very kids who fought over *not* sitting next to me couldn't get close enough to me. They struck up conversation with me, telling me that I was amazing.

It felt like some kind of cheesy 80's high school movie with a big happy ending for the nerdy kid, where the school kids lift him on their shoulders and chant his name. The closing shot starts tight on his beaming smile and zooms out as we see the crowd carrying him out of the school doors into the big bright world, all smiling faces and high fives. The musical score resolves climatically with a perfect cadence. Fade to credits.

What we rarely see in that movie is the scene three weeks later. The nerd walks through the hallway with confidence in his step, lifting his hand to give another high five to the captain of the football team. But this time he gets nothing but an eye roll. The school's excitement about the nerd dissipates as the months go on, and the chanting of his name fades into memory as the nerd finds more rejection when he goes to college, asks girls out, or interviews for jobs.

The crowd's affection, with all its adrenaline-inducing power, is a fickle and shallow drug. While I enjoyed the newfound kindness of my fellow students in that Minnesota youth group, I couldn't help but feel a slight uneasiness. I enjoyed the attention, but there was something about the whole episode that made me feel kind of dirty. I felt used.

These people don't even know me, I thought.

Fast forward another several years…

"Ten minutes until standby," a nineteen-year-old intern chirps into our green room. I nod and thank her. One of the single guys in the band says something flirty and some back-and-forth banter ensues, but I'm not listening; I'm thinking about the set.

I am about to play in front of an arena full of teenagers. We are at a Christian youth conference, and I've been asked to lead worship. I had led worship at my local church a lot, but certainly never in an arena.

The thoughts come sporadic and fast as I pace back and forth from the showers to the lockers with my guitar, absent-mindedly playing cheesy jazz licks to warm up my fingers and calm the butterflies in my stomach. The band is strapping on instruments or doing last minute hair fixes in the mirror.

It isn't long before the flirty nineteen-year-old is back. She opens the door a crack and peaks her face through with a cheesy smile.

"Alright, guys. We are ready for you."

We follow her through stark concrete hallways and into the tunnel that the basketball players walk through. As we reach the end of the tunnel, the narrow walls come to an end and the world opens up to a full arena with music pumping from huge stacks of line array speakers. The smell of hotdogs and hormones is in the air. A countdown video is playing on Jumbotron screens on each side of the stage. I hear a feisty round of "We love Jesus, yes we do! We love Jesus, how about you?" thrown back and forth between two opposing youth groups, each screaming at the top of their lungs. Evidently, they all love Jesus very, very much.

The stage manager offers some final instructions and escorts us to a ramp behind the stage. We wait in darkness as the energy in the room continues to build. The countdown draws closer to zero. My heart is pounding now.

My brother, David, is the bass player, and he is also the sports aficionado among us. He gathers us into a huddle like we are about to play for the state title. David leads us in yelling some nonsensical phrase as we put our hands into the middle and break.

We finally get the "*Go!*" from the production manager and rush up the ramp onto the darkened stage. The room has a fresh surge of volume as the audience recognizes the movement of shadows on the stage. The countdown music continues to blare, and now the clock shows thirty seconds and counting. I remember with a pang to make sure my guitar is in tune.

A few people in the audience start to chant the countdown clock—"Fifteen! Fourteen! Thirteen!—and the rest of the crowd soon joins in. "Twelve! Eleven!"

I can't see anything besides the red and yellow lights of my tuner. Oh, not now! The D string is really flat!

"Ten! Nine! Eight!"

Ah, this stupid tuner! The display keeps flashing back and forth to the wrong string! This is the D string, the D string!

I turn the tuning peg a little too hard. Now the tuner reads that my D is sharp.

"Seven! Six! Five! Four!"

Two yellow lights. Okay. I'm in tune. I'm ready. I look back at the drummer and nod my head.

"Three!"

The screaming has reached near hysterics. I can just make out the sound of the drummer clicking his sticks.

"Two!" The adrenaline-riddled crowd screams as though money is about to fall from the ceiling by the millions. The drummer starts counting off in the opposite direction: "One, two . . ."

"One!" The short breath of silence in the crowd is the eye of the hurricane. I take a breath.

The unarticulated three and four of the drummer's count-off are found in the last two clicks of his drumsticks.

The simultaneous explosion of the pyrotechnics and the eruption of the crowd signify "zero," and the band launches into full fortissimo. The lighting rig behind us rivals the suns of the Pleiades.

This was an exciting experience for a shy Midwestern boy who grew up having to drive an hour and a half to get to the town that had the Best Buy. I was the kid in the front row of a 90s Christian rock concert who was so uncool that he accidentally punched himself in the teeth while attempting the classic Arsenio Hall "Woo, Woo, Woo" rotating fist pump.

Somehow, I became the one on stage, watching as the kids in the front row screamed and pumped their fists.

When the show was done, teenagers swarmed around us. It was like they thought we were rock stars or something. Of course, we weren't rock stars. We weren't famous by any stretch of anyone's imagination. I mean, my mom has always been a huge fan, but at that time, nobody outside of the few people from our local church really knew of us at all. But at the youth conference, we had been given a place of perceived importance and power by being placed on the stage. These kids had seen our faces plastered on the giant screens. They watched as the hundred-thousand-dollar light show lit us like rock stars. The culture of this youth conference had elevated us to a position of power and prominence, and we became like the dancers from "Toymaker's Dream."

It was very strange suddenly seeing things from that perspective and hearing the voices around us give credence to the power of the stage.

"I got the bass player's signature."

"Oh, yeah? Well, Michael signed my arm."

In a fame-worshiping culture, the stage can be quite a powerful place. It can also be a dehumanizing one.

In our culture, celebrity is not the same thing as a healthy respect for the work or character of a person. Fame elevates men to gods. It turns people into objects, into desirable *things* to be photographed, prodded, touched, and consumed.

In the odd and disturbing movie *Perfume*, the protagonist develops a perfume so potently arousing to all those who smell it that he can manipulate their thoughts and desires by simply wearing a drop of it. At the end of the movie, he dumps an entire bottle over his head, and it is so unbearably attractive to the crowd around him that it brings them to a frenzy. They surround him and start clawing at him, tearing his clothes and his skin. The perfume is just too powerful, and they can't get enough of it. Eventually, they completely consume his entire body.

The greater a person's celebrity, the more we desire to know them, be near them, touch them, and consume them. We send our paparazzi to photograph their weddings and their children. We snack upon the most personal details of their lives like so much candy.

Fame is a dangerous drug for all of us. It's not only the actually famous that deal with fame-worship. We all do. Fame is a kind of subconscious currency that most of us ascribe value to. There is a reason so many people care about making the varsity team in school. It is part of the reason that first class feels so good to ride in, even though your still being forced to sit in a fairly uncomfortable chair for hours on end. It's because for a moment, you're better than *those* people in the back. You're special. You get to pee in the tiny, disgusting toilet in the front of the plane rather than the tiny, disgusting toilet in the back.

We don't like to think about this though. When we are sitting in coach, and the flight attendant closes that curtain to the first class cabin, most of us aren't marveling at the wonder of flight and thinking how fortunate we are to be traveling in a way that so few people through history have been able to do. We are mentally hurling obscenities over the curtain at those lucky bastards in the front washing their hands with those luxurious, warm washcloths. Now, of course, you have washcloths at your house. You have warm water. You *could* wash your hands with a warm washcloth a hundred times a day if you wanted to, but that's not what we're really jealous of. We are like the three-year-old kid who suddenly is not interested in his slice of chocolate cake when he sees that his big brother got a slightly bigger slice. How many creators waste their energy and emotion in comparing themselves to others? How many symphonies go unwritten because the composer is too insecure about how her work will compare to other people's work?

This kind of comparison is, like the teacher in the book of Ecclesiastes would say, meaningless, a chasing after the wind. There will always be somebody better at what you do than you are. The strongest man in the world works so hard to become the strongest man in the world. Rigorous diet, endless, grueling hours in the gym, carefully measured supplements, and so on. Yet with all of his work, an average chimpanzee is still a lot stronger than him.

When you zoom out just a little bit, the differences between human beings that we all find so important (height, weight, beauty, talent, intelligence ... etc.) start disappearing. Something my friend Andrew said recently really hit home for a guy like me who tends to think of myself as "different" or "unique." He said, "You know how everyone likes to talk about how unique every snowflake is? Well, have you ever seen a snowflake? They are actually pretty much the same. They are all tiny six-sided ice crystals."

It's true. Sure, snowflakes are unique under a microscope, but…

Snow is snow. Human beings are human beings.

There are people that spend most of their waking hours trying to knock another tenth of a second off of their hundred-meter dash. But no human being will ever be faster than a human being can be. No human being will ever be smarter than a human being can be. We are brief flashes of energy appearing for a few moments on a speck of dust in an incomprehensibly vast and mysterious universe. Yet we are so narcissistic. We think that if we could only lose that extra ten pounds and be as thin as *her* that we would be happy or at least somehow more valuable.

If I could only afford this nicer piece of technology, I could actually do something viable with my work.

If I could only…then…

Meaningless.

This is what you find when you peer into the heart of celebrity. It's empty. The kind of affirmation that we seek from others in our work is never satisfying. It is like lust. Lust has a lot of the same feelings associated with it that love does. Desire. Passion. Arousal. But lust is not love. Lust is a cheap and shallow counterfeit of love that never satisfies the soul and only quiets the body for a moment. The pleasure and joy that comes from indulged lust is temporary and fleeting, but a life of true love is the richest and most satisfying life possible. In the same way, the feeling of worth and importance that comes with the accolades of others is shallow and short-lived.

How quickly the beloved pastor becomes the hated pastor when news of his affair surfaces. The pastor was not loved so much as the idea of what people thought he was. When he falls short of the image that they have made of him, he is of no use to them anymore. They feed his carcass to the wolves.

How quickly the press spreads the "news" of the offensive comment or tasteless wardrobe decision or the extra ten pounds hanging over the bathing suit of the celebrities we claim to love. We think we adore these human beings, but we've never even met them. What we love is the idea of these people. Celebrities represent the power and love that we want for ourselves, and when they have the audacity to reveal that they are just as human as the rest of us, we're delighted to see them punished for it.

The History of Celebrity

This crazed devotion to the idea of celebrity has not always existed. Most cultures in the history of the world didn't even have the concept of celebrity. In *A Short History of Celebrity*, English historian Fred Inglis outlines the development of the idea of celebrity over the last two and half centuries, arguing that "celebrity has largely replaced the archaic concept of renown." While celebrity is focused on the looks or work of an individual, "[R]enown brought honour to the office, not the individual, and public recognition was not so much of the man himself as of the significance of his actions for the society."

Inglis claims that people like Queen Elizabeth I, author Dr. Johnson, or journalist John Wilkes were among the first people to experience the beginnings of the glory of celebrity. Then something happened in the early twentieth century that launched the worship of celebrity to a whole new level—namely, Hollywood. In the movies, people now could have an up-close and intimate view of these beautiful and talented celebrities. Before Hollywood, people might be famous by reputation, but now, on the big screen, you could stare into the faces of people like Rock Hudson or Marilyn Monroe as if you were their lover. The idea of a "star" was born.

Today, everything is so affected by the idea of celebrity that its very difficult to notice how widespread it is. Celebrity is at the foundation of why so many people do what they do. It's at the core of how we view and understand people and their art. How do you separate the music of the Beatles from their fame? Did the girls who would scream and faint when Michael Jackson walked by them do so out of a respect for his art or a worship of his celebrity? For most, it was probably a mixture of both, but how do you even start to separate which is which?

In our culture, fame sells art more than quality sells art. Jessica Simpson didn't sell twenty million albums because she is in the top tier of musical talent. She sold twenty million albums largely because she is famous. If Jessica Simpson pushed "Record" on her phone, passed gas, and put it up for sale on iTunes, she would sell more "records" of that than my band has ever sold of anything. Why? Because she is famous.

For today's artists, the primary method of success is not the quality of their work, but the marketability of their persona. You can craft a beautiful and original piece of art, but your best chance of selling it may come from wearing pants that shoot sparks out of your private parts.

If you want to get signed by a record label, one of the primary questions they will ask is, "Who is your audience?" In other words, how famous are you? How many fans do you have that we can capitalize on? Most labels aren't signing people primarily because of the quality or craftsmanship of the music, but as a wager on how famous they think you are or can become. The bulk of the budget that they will spend on you is not on the development of your music, but on the development of your brand and image. Videos, television appearances, and press releases will be the heart of your workload.

Your art is an afterthought. Your celebrity is everything.

So what is a creator to do in such an environment?

What was I supposed to do when the teenagers swarmed around me in the parking lot? Ignore them? Preach to them about how the idea of celebrity is shallow and meaningless at its best and dehumanizing at its worst? No, I think what is important here is awareness. When the creator sees the illusion of fame for what it is, it loses its power over him. So when I stand in line to take my picture with my man crush Chris Thile (which I have and would again), I recognize the absurdity of the scenario. I try not to let my respect for his work trump my ability to see him as an actual human being that deserves respect and courtesy.

And if I'm ever on the other end of that line, I gladly sign the autographs and take the pictures, because that's simply the logistical limitations of one person trying to have some sort of connection to a lot of people in a short amount of time. But I also recognize the absurdity of it. I recognize that the length of the line does not give me any more or less value as a human being. It is what it is. Celebrity exists in our culture. We can't do anything about that. But we would all do well to see it for what it really is: meaningless, a chasing after the wind.

9. RELIGION: SEXILY SHAPED MANNEQUINS

I do want everyone to feel comfortable.
That's why I'd like to talk to you about Jesus.
—Jim Gaffigan, comic

"Religion" isn't one of the most popular words right now. There are too many bad associations with it—corrupt priests, charlatans on late night Christian television, closed-minded bigotry, holy wars, and so on. Even within religious circles, people try to avoid the word. In an attempt to circumvent it, some might describe themselves as "spiritual but not religious." Others tout how they don't have a religion, just a "relationship with God."

There is a common pejorative and perhaps oversimplified assumption that all religion is nothing but dead rote rooted in superstition or mindless belief in some sort of unquestionable authority. But like art, religion is not something easily definable. The lines that divide words like religion, spirituality, faith, or philosophy can get blurry because these disciplines are often trying to answer the same questions. Why are we here? Does life have any meaning? Is there such a thing as good or evil? And whether or not we consider ourselves religious, we all have fundamental beliefs about the nature of the universe—some sort of framework of approaching the world around us.

Religious belief is kind of like sexual orientation—everyone has it. Even *not* having a preference *is* a preference in itself.

The statement "There is no God" is every bit as much of a religious statement as 'There is a God." All of us have religious beliefs and non-beliefs. Even with the increasing suspicions and doubts about organized religion in our culture, most people still claim to adhere to a certain religious system.

According to the U.S. Religious Landscape Survey, 78.4% of Americans identify themselves as "Christian."

All of the "other" faiths, such as Judaism, Buddhism and Islam, make up only about 4.7 percent of the U.S. population.

Only 1.6% identify themselves as Atheists. 2.4% label themselves as Agnostic. 12.1% believe "nothing in particular."

Most of us profess some sort of faith, but even the 12.1% who profess to believe "nothing in particular" are adhering to a belief system of sorts. They share a belief with millions of other people that no system or religious doctrine that they have come across is worth believing. It is a belief in skepticism.

Belief is inevitable, and what we believe about the world has profound effects on how we create in that world.

Of all the roots discussed in the book thus far, this one is particularly important to me personally. My religious beliefs have always had an overt and direct influence on my music. In the conservative environment in which I was raised, the lines for acceptable art had been clearly laid out. I was led to believe that if I wanted my art to be pleasing to God, it needed to fit into a set of narrow and utilitarian boxes.

Good art was that which preached a perceived Christian message or had practical use in a worship service. Art had no value in itself. There was no room in my belief system for experimenting or pushing creative boundaries. As a result, my art stayed safe, stale, and boring (by my current standards anyway).

Because my art was so directly and severely limited by my religious beliefs for so long, I have a particularly strong desire to help people tend to this root in a healthy way. I have experienced what it is like for my beliefs to imprison my soul, and I have experienced what it is like for my beliefs to set my soul free.

Of course, I do recognize that my situation was probably not the norm. Most people probably haven't attended church youth group with "secular" music destroying parties. But even though most people haven't grown up in the same kind of fundamentalist environment that I did, all creators are influenced by our religious (un)beliefs on one level or another.[1]

The artist needs faith. As I will discuss in chapter eleven, our faith gives structure to work. It is breath. It is skeleton. It is vision. Still, with belief systems comes a danger for the artist—the danger of fundamentalism.

---

1   This is part of why I have a problem with labeling only some kinds of art as "sacred," "religious," or "Christian." All art is an expression of the soul, an expression of faith. All art is sacred. All art is religious. And no art is Christian.

Fundamentalism is rigid and certain—like a prison. It leaves no room for doubt, no room for exploring or creating outside of the acceptable boxes. It is the polar opposite of creativity, the enemy of art. Fundamentalism is not limited to traditional religions like Christianity or Islam—there are fundamentalists in every stream of thought. There are fundamentalist atheists whose worldview is rigid with certainty. Even the "nothing in particular" belief can become dogmatic and arrogant. The fundamentalist's worldview is one that is not open to the unexpected or the new. It is a closed system.

Fundamentalism is not the same thing as healthy faith. Healthy faith is a gift held in open hands. There is humility in this kind of faith, a hope, an acknowledgment of the possibility of error and the need for growth and change. This openness leaves room for creativity. Fundamentalism, on the other hand, holds beliefs with a clenched fist. Fundamentalism is rooted in arrogance. It thrives in fear and control and darkness. Fundamentalism runs planes into buildings and straps bombs to the chests of devout and gullible young men. Fundamentalism divides people into groups of "us" and "them." It wages wars, systemizes racism, censors expression.

Healthy faith, on the other hand, is responsible for some of the most beautiful human expressions and social justice in the world. Aside from creating much of the most important and nourishing art throughout history, people of faith have been responsible for feeding countless hungry people, adopting orphans, caring for widows, and negotiating peace treaties. If you go to any urban center and look for who is working there to care for the homeless of that city, you will find people of faith. Good faith makes the world a better place.

This is why fundamentalism is so abhorrent. It's a perversion of something that is supposed to be good.

There is nothing as ugly in this world as innocent beauty perverted and twisted. This is why diabolical little dolls and clowns make such scary villains in horror movies. It's also the reason why any desecration of children is so abominable to us. If children weren't so beautiful and precious, we wouldn't be quite as disgusted and horrified when violence, pornography, slavery, or other abuses are perpetrated against them.

We resist bad religion with good reason. It is faith twisted into arrogant dogmatism, hope warped with violence, love perverted into the lust of power and control. Pure and faultless religion loves, clothes, serves, and ultimately unites, while bad religion condemns, steals, oppresses, and ultimately divides.

Regardless of the content of a person's beliefs, when those beliefs calcify into fundamentalism, they will not result in a worldview that lends itself to creativity, but rather to artistic imprisonment and creative death.

Like a Cow

In my own faith tradition, there is another word that you could use for the kind of unhealthy, fundamentalist belief that is rooted in fear and arrogance—idolatry.

Alongside making and performing music, the profession I have the most experience in is lawn mowing. In high school, I mowed a lot of lawn, and that is not a sexual or drug-related innuendo. Mowing was an unfortunate career decision for a kid with fairly severe hay fever allergies, but it was work, and I was glad to have it.

One of my lawn mowing jobs was for a Chinese restaurant. The owner barely spoke English, but with his machine-gun repetition and flamboyant gestures, I could generally get the gist of what he said. Except for the time when my family was eating there and he told my mom that she was "beautiful . . . like cow" over and over again.

"What?" she would ask, face flushed, looking around the table in hope that someone would explain.

"Like cow. Very beautiful!"

"Like a cow?"

"Face, beautiful, like cow."

My mom looked at me with bewilderment, but I had nothing for her. Despite that peculiar interaction, I liked the guy and was happy to be mowing his grass. One week, after I had finished mowing the restaurant's patchy and faintly MSG-smelling backyard, I gathered from the owner's broken syllables that he was asking me if I could take care of his yard at his house that week because he was going to be out of town. I told him I'd be happy to do it.

Lawn-mowing day came, and I decided to pay a friend to help me for the day. I thought that we could get everything done faster if we just brought our own mowers and knocked it out. So with some jump ropes and a skateboard, my friend and I created a train of lawnmowers that we would drive through town. If we had driven by you that day, you would have been treated to the sight of a scrawny, shirtless, bozo-haired Hispanic kid riding on a tractor and towing a scrawny, shirtless, white kid on a skateboard, who was pulling another push mower behind him with another jump rope. That's how we lawn pimps do.

When we arrived, we needed to enter the house to get the other yard care supplies that we would need. When we walked in, we immediately noticed the large clump of glittering paraphernalia in the living room. There were all sorts of candles, rugs, and other Eastern-looking trinkets surrounding an impressively sized statue of Buddha. This guy had some sort of giant shrine in his living room.

What I did next may seem strange to the average sane person, but any readers who happened to grow up around churches where people would occasionally roll around in the aisles or talk about "Jericho Marches" will certainly understand what happened next.

I bolted out of that house as quickly as I could. You see, we didn't have a lot of Eastern religious shrines in Marshfield. I didn't know what these people did what that kind of stuff. Some kind of weird sex thing? Did they sacrifice goats on it? All I knew is that it looked like some sick kind of pagan idol worship, and I thought if I stayed too long, I'd probably open myself to demonic manifestation.

In my childhood, that's how I understood idolatry—the crafting of physical statues to worship, like the story in the Bible where the ancient Israelites crafted a golden calf to worship rather than God. In the story, God was pretty angry about that; so when I saw the statue, I freaked out a little. It's the same reason I became nervous in Catholic churches as a kid. People had warned me that all of those paintings and statues were flirting with the borders of idolatry. I didn't want to be smitten.

So, yes, I got out of that house as quickly as I could.

It's easy for me to laugh at my ignorance and idiocy now, but the worldview that I was operating out of had been handed to me, and at the time it felt legitimate.

I didn't know then that Buddhists don't actually worship Buddha statues, and I didn't understand the theological richness of the images and art that Catholics use to deepen their worship of God. I also didn't understand that I, who was so quick to call other people's religious expressions idolatrous, had plenty of idols myself.

In his book *How (Not) to Speak of God*, Peter Rollins writes:

> The term [idol] can be understood to refer to any attempt that would render the essence of God accessible [to the intellect], bringing God into either aesthetic visibility (in the form of a physical structure, such as a statue) or conceptual visibility (in the form of a concept, such as a

closed theological system).... The only significant difference between the aesthetic idol and the conceptual idol lies in the fact that the former reduces God to a physical object while the latter reduces God to an intellectual object.

Fundamentalism is a lot like idolatry because it renders truth into something stagnant and lifeless. For the Christian fundamentalist, God becomes *something* that can be understood in the mind—a conceptual idol.

Idolatry is not limited to the primitive tribes that cut themselves and sacrifice their children to false gods. You can find it on mainstream television or in Grandma's neighborhood church. Fundamentalism may be found in its rawest forms in extremist groups like Al Qaeda or Westboro Baptist Church, but it also lurks in unexpected places like university classrooms and popular blogs. Fundamentalism is rife in our culture—particularly in Christendom.

With my job, I've been to hundreds of churches all around the world. I've visited churches that meet in multi-million dollar campuses and churches that gather in huts. I've seen church parking lots filled with luxury cars, and I've talked to congregants in Africa that walked miles to come, bringing their tithes of pennies or crops. I've been to Baptist churches in the South and Pentecostal churches in the North. I've been on the stage of the biggest church in the United States and in the living rooms of some of the smallest. I've been to the Vatican and to Westminster Abby. I've been in the silence of monasteries and the coffee shops of megachurches. I've led worship in some of the most conservative Christian gatherings and hung out in the beer tents and walked the prayer labyrinths of some of the most liberal.

In my travels, I have witnessed some brilliant and inspiring representations of the Church that St. Paul called the Body of Christ. I've seen churches raise millions of dollars for grand acts of mercy in the world like building clean water wells or providing small business loans for women in third world countries. I've seen small acts of selflessness and love that wrap flesh around words like "love your neighbor as yourself." I've seen true worship and devotion expressed in creative and inspiring ways—ways that bring life and healing into the world. But, unfortunately, that is not all I have seen.

As I have looked at the modern landscape of Christendom, I've also taken in an eyeful of idols. Fragmented denominations, sects, and churches like shattered glass—nearly all of us believing that we are the ones with the firmest grip on the true God. I see this and I can't imagine that it doesn't break the heart of the one who prayed in the garden that "they would be one as you and I are one."

"I follow Paul!" we scream.

"I follow Apollos!"

"I follow Luther!"

"I follow Calvin!"

"I follow Wesley!"

I see systematic theologies casting gods that fit neatly within the walls of doctrines and systems. I see a hundred million popes huddling into a million different sects based around the pope's opinions about issues like infant baptism, speaking in tongues, women in ministry, or predestination. This seems to me like a couple getting a divorce because they could not agree on what to eat for breakfast.

Idolatry divides Christianity into a shopping mall of sects, each selling their own unique god package. Churches become like stores displaying their relevant music or practical teaching like sexily shaped mannequins. Churches advertise and put on great Sunday matinee shows to attract new customers, competing with other churches for congregants like other corporations compete for clients.

This is what happens when faith becomes a set of concepts rather than a relational way of living. A concept makes a better product than a relationship. My wife could never sell my love for her to someone else. That's not how love works. She could sell some of the engraved images of my love if she wanted to. She could sell the love letters that I've written to her over the years. She could sell the pictures of us kissing our baby girl or holding hands with each other on the beach. She could sell her engagement ring or her wedding dress, but never in a million years could she sell my love for her. Idolatry mistakes relational love for God and neighbor with concept and formula, and the contemporary church advertises and sells the concepts and formulas. It reduces marriage to wedding rings and friendship to greeting cards.

As I look at the religious landscape, I see men with titles attempting to parse and carve an infinite God into little idols that fit comfortably on our denominational altars like products on store shelves—like a cow made of gold.

People have always tended to prefer dealing with religious trinkets than with infinity. Idolatry will always be poor ground to create from. It may have the power to start wars and denominations, it may have the power to inspire racism or genocide, but idol-laden religion will never make for good poetry.

10. GARDENING: WHAT DO WE DO WITH THESE ROOTS?

We could look at many other roots of the American tree that produces our art and culture, but my intention here is to begin to foster awareness, not to offer an exhaustive analysis. We could also look at the many healthy aspects of our tree— Americans have deep roots in a love of adventure, a pioneering spirit, and great courage in the face of adversity. We inherited those good roots from the people who came before us, and we've cultivated them well. In fact, the very impetus to speak freely and critique the systems of the "powers that be," which makes a book like this possible, is enshrined in both our laws and our hearts.

Other roots in our tree have allowed us to forge ahead artistically and create new sounds, mediums, technologies, and ideas that are changing the world. Our values and passions have allowed us to build creative industries that have shaped the world. What Americans have done with film, for instance, no one else has ever done. Certainly, plenty of garbage comes out in our theaters every weekend, but there are also incredible films that awaken the human heart and remind us of our deepest loves, fears, and desires, and that, all in all, make this world a better place.

I want to neither attack American culture nor romanticize it, but rather to encourage a deeper engagement and awareness of the roots of our art. If we are more mindful of what lies beneath the films that move us, the music that scores our lives, the books that help build our worldviews, and so on, our eyes will be wider and more alert, and we'll be saved from cultural and artistic imprisonment. When we learn to engage in the ordering of creation with more awareness and intention, we become less like moths simply attracted to the brightest light and more like people who are fully awake, fully engaged in the joys of ordering creation towards beauty, love, and a better world.

But this task is not easy precisely due to the conditions we've surveyed so far in this book.

When a society is bombarded with stimulation from every angle, it tends to get numb. When technology supplants craft, art tends to become less human. When most every person in our society is among the richest human beings ever to have walked the face of the earth, we tend to become lazy. When capital determines all value, art tends to become cheap. When fame is more important than the value of the work, art tends to take a back seat to image. When our religious and philosophical views of reality harden into dead fundamentalism, we grow disconnected and creatively sterile.

This is what has become of the root system of the tree from which our fruit grows.

But to stop the conversation here would be stopping short because these roots are not the source of themselves. In fact, none of the roots themselves are inherently negative. The voices that give rise to the "noise" of our culture, for instance, are not bad in themselves; they just need to be listened to properly. Technology is not inherently evil; it just needs to be utilized well. It is not bad to have our needs met or to live in a society that uses money as its standard of value. It is not wrong for a person to have cultural influence or renown, and religious belief does not necessarily devolve into idolatry.

The unhealthy aspects of these root systems that we have examined do not come from the roots themselves, but from an even deeper place. Roots always draw their nourishment from elsewhere. From the soil.

Underneath these roots lies the soil of our most fundamental and primal selves. This is the place where we hold our most basic views of reality. These views are probably not as articulate and coherent as our professed religious or philosophical systems. This is not the place of mathematical proofs or systematic theology but the raw, primordial soup of our existence. This is the place that holds our most basic fears, needs, and desires—the place that gives rise to instinct and passion. This is the soil of our humanness that makes up the ground from which all of our thoughts, words, actions, and creation spring. The Freudian might call it the Id. The mystic might call it the soul or the spirit. Whatever you'd like to call it, this deeper place affects our creativity in the most fundamental ways.

Capitalism is not to blame for the artist that panders his art for the sake of money. He panders because deep down he is afraid. He creates as he does because he is the man that he is—because he loves the things he loves and hates the things he hates. Capitalism just becomes the means by which his deepest beliefs, doubts, instincts, passions, and desires filter themselves into the external world.

Any true reformation of our creative output can only come from how we engage with the deepest places of our personhood.

Unless something of this soil can change, our creative output will remain the same. We will never be free as creators. We will always be imprisoned to our own phobias, cultural conditioning, and animal instincts—churning out predictable creative fodder like programmed machines or trained monkeys.

The soil in which we're grounded is our very humanness. And the nutrients that feed it are vast.

Water, nitrogen, oxygen, eroded stone and mineral, organic matter, rocks, thorns and weeds—soils are varied and complex. So are we. We live entwined with this mixed bag of muscle, fat, sinew, synapse, chemical, and bone raging with hormones and instincts, thoughts and emotions. Some of what makes us who we are is beyond our control. We cannot reprogram our DNA. We cannot change the fact that we need food, water, or shelter to survive. We cannot rid ourselves of our desires for love, comfort, or sex. But we can manage these desires. We can decide which of our instincts and impulses we will act on and create from. We may not be able to change the world that our eyes see, but we can move ourselves to see it from another perspective.

The Serenity Prayer asks: "God, grant me the serenity to accept the things I cannot change, courage to change the things I can, and wisdom to know the difference."

As a creator, I may never be able to paint well. I may never be able to radically change the tone or range of my vocal chords. Regardless of how hard I may wish for it, my face will never be Brad Pitt's face. I always will have grown up in Wisconsin, and I will never have a legitimate British accent. These facts are all part of what makes me who I am. As a creator, it is useless to fight this or pretend that I am not who I am. It would behoove me to instead find the serenity to accept the things that I cannot change about myself and to find ways of using my individuality to its full potential.

Still, there are a few things I actually can change about myself.

I can change what I let my thoughts dwell on. I can change what I say. I can change what I do.

That's pretty much it. That's all we human beings have control of.

I cannot decide what to be passionate about. I can pretend. I can feign excitement, trying to get myself worked up about something, but that kind of passion will only last for a moment. My true passions are too deeply ingrained in me to change them by mere willpower.

I cannot decide what I want to be afraid of. I cannot choose my deepest desires. Even my beliefs are beyond my control to a certain extent.

Before the Arminians form a protest group, let me explain.

There are at least three different ways that a person can believe in something.

1. Professed belief
2. Felt belief
3. Lived belief

As we have already seen, most of us do profess certain beliefs. In the community that I belong to, we all stand up and say old creeds together. We say things like, "We believe in one God, the Father, the Almighty, maker of heaven and earth, of all that is, seen and unseen." This is professed belief, and it is not always the same thing as felt belief or lived belief. All of us in the room may stand there professing that Jesus is Lord, and some of us may even feel like that is true. Saying the words may bring tears to some of our eyes because we really do believe them to be true. This is felt belief. A few of us may even put that belief into action, caring for widows and orphans in their distress, loving our neighbor as ourselves.

But most of us that profess Jesus as Lord live like Jesus was wrong. With our spending habits, we oppress the poor and reward the strong. We are as indifferent to our neighbors as we our to our own souls. This is lived belief.

As human beings, we have control of our professed belief. That's something that we can say. We have control over our lived belief. That's something that we can do. But we do not necessarily have control over our felt beliefs.

As hard as I may try, I will never be able to feel a belief in Santa Claus. I could *choose* to believe in him by setting out cookies for him on Christmas Eve. I could sit by the cookies and pretend that I am waiting for him to slide down the chimney at any moment. But I won't be able to expect his arrival. I won't be able to feel an emotion of gratitude toward him for my presents, because deep down, I will always know that they didn't come from him. I could start a group to spread the message that Santa Claus is real, but my heart could never be in it because deep down I believe too deeply in physics. I can see too clearly that it is not physically possible to visit every home in the world in a night. I know that the presents under the tree were purchased by me, wrapped by me (or those blessed ladies at the gift-wrapping station at the mall during the holidays), and placed under the tree by me. There simply is no room in my felt worldview for an immortal fat man in a red suit who travels around the world on a sleigh pulled by even-toed ungulates. As hard as I may try, I have no control of that level of belief.

Mahatma Gandhi asked the question, "Are creeds such simple things like the clothes which a man can change at will and put on at will?" The answer, of course, is no. We cannot change our deepest beliefs by sheer willpower.

On the surface, this is all seems a bit depressing and fatalistic. But what I have discovered in my own journey is that some of these deep primal places in us actually can change.

A person may have a rational (professed) belief that hoarding his money is not the way to live. He might have a felt belief that contradicts that rational and professed belief. He might feel the heavy hand of greed clutching at his chest. He may feel safer when he hoards his money, or may fear that if he is generous with his possessions that everything in his life will spiral out of control. He should not feel guilty about this. Whether he feels these fears or not is largely out of his control. What is in his control is how he spends his money. And over time, he may find that a consistent generosity will actually result in a changed felt belief as well. In the process of letting go of some of his possessions, perhaps he will find himself letting go of some of his fear as he finds out that even when he is generous, he still has enough. Over time, and with the right practices, some of his deepest feelings and instincts can change.

The creator who desires to tend his soil must have a little patience. Fruit, trees, roots and soil don't change overnight. It starts with a little water. A little sunlight. To clean up an unhealthy soil happens one stone, one weed at a time. This kind of change takes time. But to the creator paralyzed by unhealthy roots and phobias, imprisoned within bad faith or dark desires, there is hope. You *can* change.

In the final section of this book, I would like to explore four nutrients that I believe are important for the creator's soil. Just as a tree cannot grow without the proper nutrients, I believe that without these nutrients, our work of creativity will devolve into mindless instinct and creative imprisonment.

These four nutrients are faith, doubt, hope, and love.

PART 3 SOIL

11. FAITH: FOOLS SHINE LIKE GODS

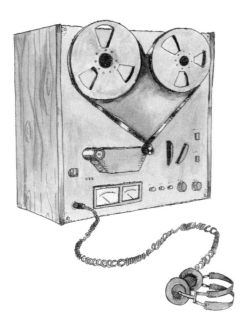

A tale of two artists:

Artist One is a brilliant photographer who professes to believe in God. He speaks about all things being beautiful and connected. But under all of the fancy language, he sees the universe as a dangerous place. A place of lack. Deep down, he believes that at the end of the day, he must look out for himself because the weak will always fall prey to the strong. His photography reflects this fear. He never takes any risks. Photography gigs are his bread and butter, so he doesn't believe that he has the luxury of exploring the outer fringes of his creativity. The universe is too dangerous for that. So his art remains safe and boring.

Artist Two is a musician who professes not to really believe in anything. Yet, deep down, he sees life as inherently good. He sees the universe as a place of abundance, not a place of lack. As a result, he sees his music as somehow very sacred. He is not able to make a living doing it full time, but he is extremely passionate about his work. Here is a letter he sent me this week about wanting to try to make an album in the near future:

Dear bros,
I want to make my record with you guys.
I don't know how it's going to happen,
but I really want it to.

I want to go to somewhere in the wilderness
bring some analog gear
and really pour out our hearts onto tape.

I want you guys on the record
because I feel safest with you,
and know I can just be totally me
and be completely unrestrained.

You guys all understand the "anointing"
and what it's like to play together
and connect
and reach something spiritual.

I'm hoping for seven days (two days setup/fun/connection/ spiritual retreat stuff, five days tracking),
with all of us there
totally engaged,
connected,
hearts out,
sharing fears
and doubts
and stuff we never feel comfortable enough to talk about

with total freedom,
only love,
no judgment,
in the wilderness.
As men.

With no ego
or want for success,
only love
and connection
and beauty
and spirituality.
I think you get the point.
love,
Rob [Wolfjaw]

Our deepest beliefs about the universe filter their way up through the soil into the tiny aesthetic decisions that the artist makes. How we make our records. Which color feels right. Rhyme schemes and word choices. These kinds of decisions are rarely made out of purely analytical comparison. They come from the guts. From faith.

Swimming upstream doesn't come naturally. If you see someone swimming upstream, you can be confident that he or she has a reason for it. This is faith. Faith is the fuel that powers unnatural endeavors. It is far easier to just go with the flow—to create in the way that your cultural roots dictate. To make work that transcends the lazy, numb, bored, and uninspiring art that is the natural course of things, one must purposefully turn around and swim upstream. To do so takes courage. Purpose. Faith. Why bother after all?

The best creating always involves pain. Late nights. Early mornings. Sore muscles. Weary, burning eyes. Why go through the pain of crafting every single word in the screenplay when the masses will probably be happy with whatever clichéd crap you throw at them? Why bother speaking up against the system when the system is so much bigger and stronger than you? Why not just fall in line and do as everyone else is doing?

Only the person with healthy faith knows the answers to these questions. Even if the answer is only a vague and frustrated "Because!" the person of faith knows that it is worth it. She feels it in her bones.

This kind of passionate faith can be painful. Not caring is easy. Caring hurts. Caring costs you something. But without this sort of faith, you will never create to your fullest potential.

Faith is a gift. Like I've said, felt belief is not necessarily something that you choose to have or not to have. But it is a gift that you can open yourself to receive. The writer cannot choose whether or not the inspiration will strike, but he can show up to his computer every morning. Still, how does the writer find the inspiration to set his alarm to wake up in the morning? How does he open his word processor and wait for the words to come rather than playing video games or browsing his ex-girlfriend's pictures on Facebook? Even this simple exercise of discipline takes a degree of faith. So how does one receive faith? Here, we come back to the idea of *listening*.

Faith comes from listening to the right stories.

After all, if you dig into the soil of our humanity, what will you find there?

More than skin and bone, muscle and tendon—you are made of stories.

The physicality of a human being is always changing. Every single cell in the human body regenerates every seven to ten years. This means that on a cellular level, you have a completely different body than you did a decade ago. But of course, we are the same person because regardless of our physicality, there is something about an individual human being that stays consistently, uniquely, and utterly himself or herself. That something is story.

Atoms come and go. Cells will be born and they will die. We'll shed our skin. Our hair will fall out. We can gain weight, lose weight, break bones, get organ transplants, but in themselves, these things do not affect our personhood. Our stories do.

Beliefs are stories.

We like to put labels and big fancy capital letters on our belief systems. Secular Humanism. Hinduism. Christianity.

But most often, these labels don't actually mean very much because people within the same labels can believe vastly different stories.

Some Buddhists believe that a higher power created the world; some do not. Some scientists believe that evolution is the result of a cold, dead, random universe. Others believe that there is some higher force or God involved in the process of evolution. One evangelical Christian preacher teaches that only evangelical Christians go to Heaven. Another will teach that no one goes to a place called Heaven, but that Heaven is a dawning way of life on the earth and is certainly not limited to evangelical Christians.

People within the same label can believe vastly different stories. And people that believe the same stories can see those stories from any number of perspectives.

So forget about your label for a moment—whether you are a Catholic or an Orthodox Jew or a New Atheist. What are your most important stories? These stories lie at the heart of what you believe, how you behave, and what you create.

A person that is afraid of dogs is most likely not that way because of exhaustive scientific inquiry or logical analysis but because of experience. They have stories of dogs harming people.

Our stories are everything we have. Our relationships are stories. (Strangers are people that we have no stories with.) Families are stories. None of our possessions would mean anything to us without stories. This is why we spend trillions of dollars on stories. Films. Books. Magazines. Newspapers. Websites. Advertising. Religion. It all comes down to stories.

The creator cannot control the stories she experiences, but with a cultivated awareness, she can adjust her perspectives of them. She can recall and dwell on the stories that she chooses to.

As a creator, I have found that how I engage with the stories that I have experienced makes all the difference in the world for how I create. I still have the story of the botched vocal solo in my junior high play burning bright in my memory, but I've decided not to build my behavior on that story. After four years of letting that experience paralyze my creative expression, I had to stop dwelling on that memory if I wanted to move forward. I had to let that story fade into the background and let the foreground teem with stories that are more inspiring to create from.

The Homeless Jew

The primary reason I create what I create today is because of a story that I grew up listening to. A story of lost things being found, of injustice appealed and set to rights. It is lions laying with lambs and swords beaten into plowshares. It's a story of graves with empty bellies and of a God who kissed the broken earth with a future heaven. We called this story the Gospel, or the Good News.

In this story, I heard about how cowardly fishermen found the courage of martyrs. I heard about a greedy and despised tax collector who suddenly decided to give all of his possessions to the poor. Over and over again, I would hear stories like the one about a woman who was caught in the act of adultery. The religious people wanted to stone her, but this homeless Jewish rabbi showed up and saved her life. These stories were all centered on this man from a small rural town in ancient Palestine called Nazareth.

This man—this Jesus—has captivated billions of people throughout twenty centuries of history.

In these stories that I grew up hearing, Jesus never had a mild effect on people. Either they hated him or they loved him. The kind of love that inspired a prostitute to barge into a party full of powerful religious leaders and humiliate herself by falling and weeping at Jesus' feet. This was not the safe Jesus who poses for photographs with baby lambs. The Jesus in these stories was a subversive, revolutionary man who ferociously overturned the tables of the moneylenders in the temple. Sinners loved him but religious people often found him very offensive. Jesus never followed their rules like they wanted him to. He kept reaching out to touch the untouchable and love the unlovable, and it drove them crazy. Those people were not the kind of people a Jewish rabbi should be spending his time with.

I grew up constantly hearing these stories, and I ended up falling in love with this Jesus. This Jesus so full of life and unbridled joy that children flocked to him; the Jesus so enrapturing that working fisherman dropped their nets to go wherever he might lead them.

In a world that so often operates by the survival of the fittest, Jesus was a man who pointed toward a radically different and emerging reality that he called the "Kingdom of God." In this Kingdom, God comes not as the one who is served, but the one who serves. Jesus taught of a present/future reality where the oppressors do not have the last word, where power and victory are not measured by the sword, but by love. All of this flew directly in the face of their empire, which was ruled entirely by the sword.

Then there was the story of Jesus on the cross. My heart would ache as I listened to the story of how the Roman Empire condemned Jesus to death row as an enemy of the state, brutally murdering him on a cross. There was something so tragically true to life in that story.

I heard how the band of disciples that had followed Jesus through his ministry scattered in embarrassment after Jesus had been crucified. I could relate to that. How many times had I betrayed my deepest beliefs because I was afraid? The disciples had high hopes for this man from Nazareth. They had hoped Jesus would deliver them from their oppressors, the Romans. They had wanted him to take David's throne and deliver the Jews out of bondage and into power. The cross was glaring proof to them that they had been wrong about Jesus.

But then, of course, the story takes a turn. Word began to spread that Jesus had been raised from the dead.

A mixture of historical record and tradition tell the stories of what happened to the early friends of Jesus—the very friends who had scattered scared in the wake of his crucifixion. Andrew was reportedly crucified, as was Simon (although some say that Simon was actually sawn in half). Peter was crucified upside down in Rome; he apparently asked to have his head facing downward because he didn't feel worthy to die the same manner of death as his Lord. Bartholomew was either beheaded or crucified upside down. James the Greater died by the sword. James the Lesser was reportedly thrown from the Temple at Jerusalem and stoned and beaten with clubs. Jude was also apparently beaten to death with a club. Matthew was either stoned, burned, or beheaded, and Phillip was martyred as well. The only disciple who is believed to have survived the Roman persecution of these early Christians was John.

Though I've certainly had my doubts about this story, I've always wondered—why didn't anybody crack? People don't normally willingly die for something they know to be a lie. All of these early disciples claimed to have seen a resurrected Jesus. They claimed to have sat and spoken and eaten with him. Christianity spread so quickly through the world because these early Jesus followers actually believed that Jesus had been raised from the dead, and as a result they were not afraid of death anymore. They saw that the Kingdom that Jesus had always talked about had been sprouting up among them. They saw the blind receive sight, and they received sight themselves. So when the stones began to pummel them one excruciating blow at a time, piercing skin and breaking bone, when the nails plunged into their hands and the saws into their stomachs, these early believers were able to say with tears in their eyes the same words that their Lord had said: "Father, forgive them, for they know not what they do."

This story!

Because of this story, people have stared death in the face and laughed.

O death, where is your sting? O grave, where is your victory?

It is this story that has led men like Johann Sebastian Bach and George Frideric Handel to compose their music for *Soli Deo gloria* (glory to God alone). It is this story that fueled Dietrich Bonheoffer's valor in standing up against his own countrymen in Nazi Germany. This is the good news that inspired William Wilberforce to stand up for people who weren't considered fully human, that impelled Nelson Mandela to fight the system of Apartheid that was breaking the backs of the oppressed. This is the story that nourishes the pen of Annie Dillard as she writes such honest and eloquent prose:

> I am a frayed and nibbled survivor in a fallen world, and I am getting along. I am aging and eaten and have done my share of eating too. I am not washed and beautiful, in control of a shining world in which everything fits, but instead am wondering awed about on a splintered wreck I've come to care for, whose gnawed trees breathe a delicate air, whose bloodied and scarred creatures are my dearest companions, and whose beauty bats and shines not in its imperfections but overwhelmingly in spite of them.

It seems to me that this story in a culture like ours should continue to be the source of great creativity and courage. Why? Because to these early believers, and to others through history, this empty tomb was the beginning of everything becoming *new*. There is a reason that the Scriptures the early believers assembled began in Genesis with creation and ended in Revelation with *new* creation. In Jesus, the source of creation bleeds his blood into our barren ground, and the soil becomes a garden of resurrection.

The empty tomb of Jesus echoes in the hearts of those who look upon it, "Death has lost its sting!" The prisons will someday empty. The rich will not always rule in oppression over the poor. This is not the end of the story. This story is not simply rooted in memory, but in imagination. The future unfolds, granting us new questions. How shall we imagine now? What shall we make? What shall become of this pregnant creation?

When freed from the weeds and thistles of idolatry and fundamentalism, I think that the story of Jesus called the Christ ought to be the most poignant and fertile of all soils in which human creativity can be planted. For the believer, this story is rooted in the ground of being itself, or in the Christian perspective, *Himself*. This soil is the Reality in which we live and move and have our being. It is in the ground of Reality in which all things are pulled into existence and held together.

While this is all very romantic and beautiful to me, I must admit that sometimes the whole thing sounds extremely naïve and foolish. Some days, the creeds that I confess with my community of faith ring flat in my ears or sound like any other myths or legends through the centuries about gods and heroes and people rising from the dead.

As much as I may love the story and desire to believe it, there are times when I can't. There are times when I try to pray, but my felt belief won't cooperate. It feels like I am talking to the air.

I asked my wife recently if she would still love me if I were a bald atheist. She said she would, which was a relief. I'm not an atheist, nor am I bald, but I do take hair loss medication and have a lot of doubt.

Still, there seems to be something living within these stories and creeds that has gripped my soul. It's as though there are hands wrapped around my very heart, and as much as doubt or scientific analysis tries to wrench the hands free, there is no use. I have been marred by this story of a marred Messiah.

So I keep coming back and listening to the story. That's why I am still part of the community with the weird mountain people in Colorado. I sometimes look around, seeing the company of others who claim the same foolishness as I, and I want to turn around and run out of this party of broken fools. But then I turn back and it's as if I can see the smiling eyes of the one who invited me. I squirm and doubt my very faculty of vision. Surely, I must be imagining this. This is neurons and synapses gone awry. But then the Bread that was dipped in the Wine touches my lips, and the scales fall from my eyes and the broken fools shine like gods. I see Reality and my heart beats to life.

I'm an addict. I can't stop coming back to the Table. Nor do I want to.

When I plant myself in the ground of this story, I am more alive, more creative. I feel freer to imagine and form creation toward a future of unlimited possibility—like an Adam in a garden who has been handed the infinite, raw potential of a becoming world and invited to sculpt and name and play.

In this story, my imagination is set free as it envisions the earth as part of the creation that will someday be set free from its bondage to decay. This is a framework in which one can anticipate the arrival of Beauty's fullness. Here, art is not simple ego inflation or therapeutic emotional expression—it is connected to the very source and essence of all life. It brings into fulfillment the ultimate hope of the world for renewal. It is the anticipatory painting of a room that will eventually be lived in. It is the present feeding and clothing of those who are to eventually be clothed and fed. Art is not a distraction from human meaninglessness, but part of burgeoning newness that gives our existence a hopeful and sacred meaningfulness.

This is not the escapist Christianity that Marx justifiably railed against; in fact, this story speaks of the opposite of escapism. It speaks of incarnation. It is a future hope taking root in the present. It is a view that the Creator has not given up on his creation and an invitation to join in the sculpting of creation's dirt into something that God might breathe his very breath into. As LeRon Shults writes in *Reforming the Doctrine of God,* "[H]ope is not merely patiently waiting for utopia, but a way of relating to the future that transforms reality now."

So I listen to this story again and again. I let it do its work in the places that I can't reach on my own. In a culture numbed and indifferent from overstimulation and noise, this story begins to infuse life and feeling back into my limbs, awakening my senses with the anticipation of new creation. It begins to enliven my dulled imagination with new color and possibility. In this story, technology becomes just another tool to order creation towards that future where God is all and in all—where tears are wiped away and mankind is in perfect communion with that all.

In a capitalistic culture, the Gospel that is based in love and the giving of oneself begins to reveal the love of money for the illusion that it is. This story breaks open the prisons of consumption and greed and sets us free into a new world where material resources become like a paintbrush in the hand of an artist, painting the colors of heaven on the canvas of earth— widows and orphans cared for, God's good world ordered, stewarded, and protected.

For me, Jesus exposes the altar of fame as the dehumanizing idol that it is. In this story that values every human being as equally sacred and important, I can see the illusion of celebrity for what it is. Here, there is no hierarchy of humanity. There is no more Jew nor Greek, male nor female, slave nor free, famous nor ordinary, black nor white, gay nor straight, Christian nor secular. In the Gospel, all are endowed with the image of their Creator, and all are called to the Table. The Gospel unfolded reveals one new humanity in the making. A new humanity invited into a new creation.

And bid our sad divisions cease.

It wasn't always like this, though. In fundamentalism, my religious beliefs had precisely the opposite effect. Rather than inspiring creativity, the story inspired fear. Rather than being the hope of all things being made one in God, the story had somehow become about me. Me getting to heaven. Me being right.

The sad truth is that the sort of Christian faith that can be a rich soil for creative endeavor is not nearly as visible or practiced within our society as other sorts are. Much of Christendom has devolved into a dead fundamentalism. Like a rose choked by thorns. Like a once fertile soil made barren with stone and weeds. And when good soil is cluttered and choked, one must plow before one can expect to gather a harvest.

This is how it is with all our beliefs and stories, not just the religious ones. The fundamental beliefs about ourselves and the world around us are often so warped by our personal experiences and egos that they can become very destructive. And while we may not be able to change them entirely overnight, significant change can come from just the slightest shift in perspective.

Two Inches

A few years ago, I wanted to take some guitar lessons from an accomplished classical guitarist named Ana Vidovic. Ana's playing is extremely virtuosic and impressive. I showed Lisa a video of Ana playing a piece on YouTube. Lisa's response: "No way."

"Are you kidding me? Look at her, she's amazing, and she's gorgeous! There's no way you are flying across the country to take lessons from *her*."

I laughed at her and said "Okay." (Jealousy can be pretty cute sometimes.)

But then, Lisa realized that it would be a mistake to not take advantage of an opportunity to study with someone of that caliber, even if Ana wasn't a 300-pound old hag with a patch over her eye like Lisa would have preferred her to be.

I tried to prepare some pieces to play for my lessons with Ana, but I knew as I prepared them that they didn't sound right. I practiced and practiced, but I just couldn't ever get my guitar to sound the way that I wanted it to.

When I played the pieces for Ana, she immediately saw what was wrong. It wasn't my guitar; it was my technique. My wrist was about two inches too close to the strings. As a result, the shape of my hand wasn't correct in relation to the strings. I was striking the strings at the wrong angle with the wrong part of my fingernails, and that's why my tone was so sharp. I had been able to hear that the tone was wrong. I had tried to fix it by playing softer or filing my nails differently. I had tried contorting my fingers, trying to find a way to strike the string in a way that sounded better, but Ana saw that it was much simpler than that. All I needed to do was lift my wrist a couple of inches. I did so, and the sound of my guitar changed.

Two inches.

The art that I make now is very different from the art that I made several years ago. A lot of people ask me what inspired that change. You know what the answer is? A theological lifting of the wrist. Just a couple of inches, but that slight change of posture changed everything for me.

Often the difference between a healthy root and an unhealthy one is a subtle one. There is difference between *working* for money and working *for* money. Using technology is not the same thing as being used by technology. Living in a culture of first world luxury is not the same as living with an entitlement of first world luxury. These differences may not be easily discernable to the outsider. On the surface, the differences between a strong religious devotion and an arrogant fundamentalism may not appear significant. Both the war-monger and the peace worker pray the words "Thy will be done." They sit in the same pews, recite the same creeds. (Perhaps this is why many of the anti-religious voices in our culture paint with such a broad brush—it is simpler that way.) The difference between healthy faith and idolatrous fundamentalism is a difference of posture and perspective. It comes down to issues of foreground and background. The slightest lifting of a wrist.

This is why a keen sense of awareness is so important for the creator. We are too often blind to the true implications and fruits of our beliefs. Think of a racist who tries to hide his racism by treating his black co-worker with special attention and eager smiles. The co-worker most likely still feels the racism in the forced smiles and sycophantic bumbling, but the racist gets to pretend that he is not a racist after all.

The greedy person fools himself into thinking that he is just trying to provide for his family. The fame worshipper convinces herself that she is not obsessed with celebrity; it's simply her destiny or calling to be famous.

I am convinced that most people do not really believe what they say they believe. Or perhaps I should say that it seems that most people's professed belief is not the same as their felt belief or their lived belief.

Very few of us would profess to believe that we should allow technology to take over our lives, supplanting relationships and creativity with Facebook and auto-tune. Yet, when it comes down it, we opt for the technology. Most Americans wouldn't profess that life has been tougher for us than it has been for most other people throughout history, but that doesn't mean we won't whine like it.

A healthy faith is one that has aligned in word, thought, and action. So how can the creator start to close the gap between what he says he believes and how he actually lives? How can he become aware of the stories that he has built his life on and how the stories play themselves out in his work?

One way is through doubt.

DOUBT : A MEDIUM-GRAINED NAIL FILE

When I was a kid, I went to a school that I'm pretty sure was founded mostly for me. That may be an inaccurate and grossly egocentric theory, but my dad was the pastor of the church that built the school, and it was founded a year before I was to start school. The school started in what I think may have been a trailer park, and was originally limited to K-4 through eight grade. Curiously, it expanded into high school grades the very year that I was to become a freshman.

I don't know. Sounds fishy to me.

I enjoyed Marshfield Christian School, though. It felt safe. We didn't have gangs or metal detectors. My parents didn't have to worry too much about me getting hooked on drugs or losing my virginity at twelve years old.

We would start every school day by pledging allegiance to the American flag, then the Christian flag, then the Bible, and then, for a couple of years, we even put on our spiritual armor. This consisted of a curious little action-laden chant where we did things like put on our "helmet of salvation" and our "sword of the Spirit." It ended with all of us hugging ourselves and saying, "I love myself."

In Christian school, I learned how to avoid the trappings of "the world" and stay "pure." I didn't say cuss words or listen to "secular music." I didn't date girls or watch MTV or R-rated movies (except once in a while when my dad would let me watch a movie like *Terminator 2* with him . . . which I thought was pretty much the best thing ever). All in all, I was pretty insulated from the world outside of my sterile, Christian bubble. My world was sturdy and secure.

That is, until Mr. Martin came to town.

Mr. Martin was a New Englander that moved to Marshfield to be a teacher at the newly founded Marshfield Christian High School. From the first day of class, his dry wit and strong accent made him stand out in stark contrast to his polite and slower speaking, "Yooper"-sounding colleagues. He had a tight little mop of curls on the top of his head and a thin beard that was perhaps a little too dainty for a respectable central Wisconsin man. (If you were going to have a beard in central Wisconsin, you should be able to use it to wipe the blood off of your hunting knife.)

From the start, Mr. Martin told us that we were going to have our work cut out for us that year. He let us know of his high expectations and that he would not be permissive of lazy thinking in his classes. He was going to train us to be thinkers. "Come on, think" became a Mr. Martin mantra that would last through my entire Marshfield Christian High School career.

Early on, Mr. Martin began talking about a book that he was going to have us read later in the year. It was a book that would help us to think more sharply, see the world more clearly. He was really obsessed with this book. He wouldn't go more than a couple weeks without mentioning it.

In the meantime, we studied all the normal subjects, but something was different about them with Mr. Martin. It wasn't just factual memorization and recall with him. He challenged us to interpret and analyze the material for ourselves and not to just lazily regurgitate what the page said. He gave us journals that we were required to write in every day. He taught us about spiritual disciplines and had a passion for his faith that was rare even for us "charismatics." Everything about Mr. Martin was a little strange. He owned a ram's horn, and made us sing these weird minor-keyed praise songs all of the time—like one that kept asking questions like "Where are the people of passion?" and "Where are the people of fire?" I guess the answer was supposed to be: he's up front, blowing a ram's horn.

Still, as strange as he was, I started really liking Mr. Martin. His oddness was appealing to me. I began to trust what he said, so when he kept building this book up month after month, I began to grow quite excited about it. We all did.

This book was going to reveal to us things about the world that we never knew. It was going to open our eyes to reality. The book was called *A New World Order*, and Mr. Martin's enthusiasm for it was contagious.

Finally, the day arrived and he brought the box of pale yellow booklets into the classroom. He set them down on his desk with a thud, and the excitement was palpable. He waited until the end of the day to hand out the books, so by the time I had my own personal copy placed in my hand, I doubt any fourteen year-old had ever been so excited about getting a new schoolbook.

On first glance, the book didn't look that impressive. The cover was nothing but a piece of ugly pale yellow paper with black type on it: *A New World Order*.

There were no other colors or graphics or endorsements from other authors. No mention of being a part of any sort of best-selling list. Just that cold black typewritten title that made the booklet look like some top-secret underground manual that needed to be destroyed after reading.

As soon as I got home, I began devouring the book.

As I began to read it, some of the material sounded familiar. I had heard some of these things before from preachers who had come to our church. A global conspiracy was happening and the world was moving toward having a one-world government. The European Union had recently been formed, and it, along with the United Nations and other worrying developments, was part of a massive movement toward a government that would eventually be ruled by one charismatic leader—the anti-Christ, of course.

I had been to a lot of church meetings and had heard pastors talk about this kind of thing before. I didn't know if I believed all of it, but it always scared the crap out of me.

The anti-Christ would force us to get a barcode on our hands that would identify us and allow us to purchase things. Kind of like a credit card, only it makes you go to hell.

What I was amazed to see in this book, however, was how far along these things already were. I was shocked to discover that VISA is actually a coded version of the number 666.

The author went on to reveal how the government is already starting to invade our privacy and control our lives. I was appalled to read that even my junior high term papers would be stored and coded into the magnetic strip on my credit cards.

It was all so shocking and outrageous. I didn't know how to take it. So I brought the book to my dad to see what he thought. I told him what the book was claiming and showed it to him. He looked at me incredulously.

"Mr. Martin gave you this?"

"Yeah."

"He actually believes this?"

"Yeah."

He perused it for a few moments, and then shut the book, telling me that it was exaggerated and fantastical. He was going to have to have a talk with Mr. Martin about making us read a book like this.

I must say that I was quite disappointed with his reaction. I went back to my reading in hopes that he was wrong and that the truth was just too much for him to handle. But suddenly, the book did seem pretty ridiculous. I saw that none of the "facts" were supported by any real evidence or documentation. There was no proof of any of the conclusions that the booklet claimed as unassailable secret truth. The more I read, the more apparent it was that this whole book was wild conjecture from some fruit loop conspiracy theorist. Suddenly, the pale yellow cover didn't seem as intriguing and mysterious. It was probably just the cheapest and easiest way for the author to print the books from his mom's basement.

The next morning, I stormed into class in an uproar. All I could talk to anyone about was the book and how outrageous it was. How could Mr. Martin have suggested this? He was an intelligent guy. I trusted him. We all did. A small army of protestors began to form, and when Mr. Martin finally entered the classroom, he nearly had a riot on his hands.

The protestors erupted, but to our surprise, Mr. Martin did not respond emotionally. He just sat there and smiled at our outrage. He gave us a minute, and then calmly asked us to settle down and sit so we could actually talk about it. We reluctantly consented.

He asked us to reasonably articulate what we thought of the book. We told him how we thought it just some crackpot spouting off his conspiracy theories without any proof. There was no documented evidence for his claims, and it was inappropriate material to give us under the pretense of academic legitimacy.

We expected him to fight back. We expected a flushed face or a sarcastic tirade. But he simply sat. And smiled.

"Good job, class."

Dumbstruck.

"I'm proud of you."

Slowly, awareness dawned. He had tricked us. The dainty-bearded bastard tricked us.

He knew from the beginning that the book was a load of nonsense, but he wanted us to come to that conclusion on our own. As always, he was teaching us to think. And that meant we had to question even what he taught us. It meant we had to question the questioner. To look at things in a deeper way than, "Well, Mr. Martin said it was true, so it must be."

Well played, Martin.

The problem was that I realized that I hadn't really thought for myself. I wasn't the one who initially recognized the foolishness of the book. My father had.

I felt like an idiot. I had let my trust in Mr. Martin stop me from using my mind. If I had just picked the book off of the shelf of a bookstore, I probably would have recognized it for the nonsense that it was, but because Mr. Martin had spoken so highly of it, I blindly believed it was trustworthy. It was humiliating to realize that I had needed to have my dad, who was probably the only man I respected more than Mr. Martin, help me see that it wasn't true.

And the seed of doubt was planted.

I decided that day as a freshman in high school never to just blindly believe something that authority figures tell me, even Mr. Martin, even my dad. I was going to try to look at things myself and see if they made sense on their own.

That decision has come to be a painful one. That moment was the beginning of an unraveling of certainty. A hole had been punched in the bubble, and it was no longer sterile inside. My world started getting bigger. Eventually all the stories that I believed would start being put through the ringer of doubt. I have rarely enjoyed that process, but without it, I never could have escaped the evils and limitations of fundamentalism or idolatry. My art never could have moved forward. Without doubt, I never would have taken lessons from Ana Vidovic. She never would have told me that I needed to lift my wrist. My playing would have stayed the same. Without doubt, there can be no change, no growth. Doubt asks questions that need to be asked to make our faith pure and healthy.

I've talked about how the creator needs faith. The creator also needs doubt.

In reality, there is no faith without doubt. To believe one thing is to not believe another. Faith gives structure to work, but doubt gives structure to faith. Doubt asks questions that can keep faith from becoming ignorant superstition, violent triumphalism, or destructive judgmentalism. Doubt purifies faith. Without doubt, belief calcifies into rigid fundamentalism. Without doubt, there are no questions; and without questions, there is no imagination.

Some people think that doubt and faith are polar opposites. They are not. Doubt and faith go hand in hand. One without the other devolves into fundamentalism.

Doubt helps us de-thorn the rose, but I should warn you that the process can be precarious and potentially painful. The work of weeding a garden is not always easy, but it is necessary if you want a garden that can grow.

Arrogance

We humans are so proud at how much smarter we are than other animals. We live sixteen years, and we think we have the world figured out. We live ten, twenty, thirty more years, and then we laugh about how we thought we had the world figured out "back then." But our laughing is a result of us thinking that we have a realistic grasp of the world now.

There's this passage in the book of Job where God responds to this characteristic human arrogance with outright sarcasm:

> Where were you when I laid the earth's foundation? Tell me,
> if you understand.
> Who marked off its dimensions? Surely you know!
> Who stretched a measuring line across it?
> On what were its footings set, or who laid its cornerstone—
> while the morning stars sang together
> and all the angels shouted for joy?
> Who shut up the sea behind doors
> when it burst forth from the womb,
> when I made the clouds its garment . . . (Job 38:4–9)

At least God is poetic in his sarcasm.

The Scriptures get quoted by fundamentalists so often that it's easy to associate the Bible with closed-minded arrogance. But the message of the Scriptures always flies in the face of our arrogance. In the Scriptures, we are dust (Genesis 1). We are mist (Psalm 27). We are breath and shadow (Psalm 144). Everything is meaningless (Ecclesiastes 1).

Yet somehow, in the embrace of our frailty and meaninglessness, we find meaning. This is faith. Faith is the opposite of arrogance. Faith is open eyes and open heart.

Good faith keeps us aware of our humanness. So does science.

If you stretch out your arms and imagine that your wingspan represents the timeline of earth's history, how long do you think humans have been around? One arm length? Nope, shorter. A hand? A finger? Nope. According to John McPhee in *Basin and Range*, a single swipe from a medium-grained nail file to the end of your middle fingernail would eradicate all of human history from the 4.5 billion years of earth's history.

If a person eats his vegetables, stays active, and gets lucky, he might live to be a hundred years old. Where was man when the dinosaurs roamed the earth? Where was he when the moon got caught into earth's gravitational pull? He doesn't know all that much about this tiny little rock that we live on, let alone the hundreds of billions of solar systems in our galaxy, which is just one of hundreds of billions of galaxies in the known universe.

Arrogance is folly.

Doubt is the artist's friend because it helps us move beyond our narcissistic arrogance. It allows for imagination, for new possibilities. What if Albert Einstein had never doubted the scientific assumptions of his time? What if Stravinsky had never wondered if there was more musical terrain to explore than he had been taught? What if he had been comfortable with the boundaries that had been presented to him?

Most of the great artists and innovators through history experience a degree of cognitive dissonance within their worlds and worldviews. If they didn't, they wouldn't put so much effort into changing the world around them. The greatest artists are never fundamentalists. Creativity cannot thrive without some measure of doubt.

I'm not saying that doubt is easy. It's not. It's terrifying. Nor am I encouraging people to casually throw away their beliefs for the purpose of being artistic. What I am doing is encouraging an open heart and an open mind—a cultivation of faith that purified by doubt, a faith that is more than mere arrogant certainty or strict mental assent to a set of ideas, but rather a living and breathing movement toward truth, toward reality. It is here than we can learn to become human in the fullest sense. It is here that we can start to create out of some very rich and nourishing soil.

13. HOPE: A SINGLE GRAIN OF SALT

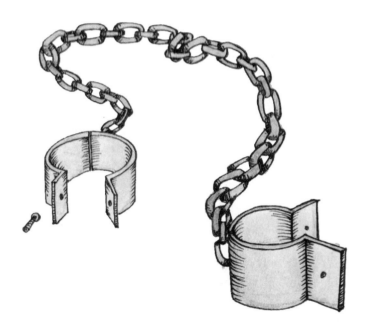

I started this book by talking about how my burnout inspired me to take a spiritual retreat. My destination for that trip was Assisi, Italy. I arrived in Assisi on a Sunday night in September and was greeted by a woman who looked to be in her early fifties. Her name was Ruth. She wore baggy, robe-like clothing and welcomed me in a whispery voice. She ushered me through a garden and to my room. No TV. No On-Demand service. No phone or small business center. Just a bed.

On my bed was a small packet of information including our daily schedule for the retreat, which went something like this:

1. Wake up, get ready, and eat breakfast in silence
2. Group meditation for an hour
3. Group prayer movements
4. Silent lunch
5. Personal silence and meditation (optional trip to other meditation sites)
6. Silent dinner
7. Evening group meditation
8. Sleep

I'm not an extroverted person most of the time, so I thought I would be comfortable with a lot of silence. But I wasn't prepared for the shock of being submerged into total silence for a week. At first, the silence felt heavy. It was awkward to not speak to these strangers that I was suddenly living with.

I would sit there at the same table with someone face to face, hearing every movement he made—the sound of cereal being crunched, noodles being stirred, chewing and swallowing—all while not being able to say a word to make the silence less awkward. It was a full embrace of the awkward.

After breakfast, we would join Bruce and Ruth, the hosts, in the meditation room. The retreat was not labeled as Christian but "inter-religious." The room had statues of the Virgin Mary next to a Buddha next to a Hindu something or other. But since we weren't talking to each other, I had no idea whether the people in the room were Christian, Muslim, Jew, Atheist, or anything else. We didn't know how much money each other made, what kind of political positions we adhered to, or what kinds of music we preferred. We were all just human beings, and that was very refreshing for me at the time.

We'd meditate for an hour in silence. At the beginning of the session, Bruce would say something ambiguous and confusing like, "Today we are going to spend time with lady poverty. We will go now into our hearts and sink into the ocean of our retreat." I didn't really know what he was talking about, but I did enjoy how he spoke in a nice, soothing tone. Then we were just thrown headlong into the quiet.

We would sit there for an hour at a time in complete silence. There was no spa music, no church altar call keyboard pads to fill the all-consuming silence. Only the grumblings of bellies and the shifting of sore spines.

The first day of this was especially difficult. It felt like I was a can of water that had been rolling down a hill and this retreat was a curb that violently stopped the rolling. The can had come to an abrupt halt, but the liquid inside kept rolling around. On the outside, we were all sitting in slowness and silence, but the pace of life inside of me had not changed yet. Thoughts came quickly and randomly. I couldn't focus. I couldn't stop from shifting in my seat and feeling bored. As the retreat progressed, however, my internal world began to calm down and line up with my outer actions.

Time slowed down. The quiet became more comfortable, then peaceful and even healing. After a few days, I started to wonder why people talk so much. What is it about silence that we are so afraid of? I looked at normal human interaction and conversation and saw how much fear and self-consciousness were present in nearly all of these interactions. We fill the silence with noise because we don't want to be perceived as boring. We are afraid the other person will feel uncomfortable or think less of us, so we do our best to fill every second of space. Noise like fig leaves sewn together to hide our true humanness. We want people to perceive us as smart, funny, or interesting, so we sew our fig leaves and avoid the silence that places us all at the same level of simply being.

Bruce told us in his soft, soothing voice at the end of our first meditation session that if any of us wanted to speak with him in a short counseling session, this would be a permissible break in our silence. This took Bruce about a minute to say, because Bruce speaks about a word a second. Not. Very. Fast.

I tried to talk to him the first day. I told him with fast words about some of my angst about being associated with the Christian music industry. Despite the good that I have experienced in the industry, and as much as I had loved making music that reflected my faith, I told him that I felt like I didn't believe in a lot of the things that seemed to be foundational to the some of the industry's very existence. I told him that I was uncomfortable with some of the boxes that I felt people wanted me to fit into, and that I didn't know whether continuing to make music in my industry was somehow hypocritical. If I had so many problems with it, was that a sign that I shouldn't be in it? I felt like my doubts and questions somehow disqualified me from being part of it. I told him I was thinking about quitting. Certainly, there are other people more qualified to do this. I'm just a doubting flounderer trying to make some decent and honest music.

Bruce smiled at me with that goofy smile of his, his wrinkly, droopy eyes staring unflinchingly into mine. Bruce spent a lot of time meditating, and wasn't afraid to look you in the eye for a while. He said a few encouraging words, and then just sat there staring at me unflinching and goofy-smiled. I eventually just thanked him and went back outside, making a mental note not to schedule any more counseling sessions with Bruce.

I realized later that perhaps he realized that what I needed was not more words. Bruce could not fix me. All he could do was encourage me to rest and let go of my anxiety. In the silence, the answer would present itself.

After my short meeting with Bruce, it was time for prayer movements.

Ruth was a little less spacey than Bruce, but she was an interesting bird herself. She led us in the movements, and at first, I was kind of nervous. I did P90x for a little while, but aside from that, I've never been a yoga meditation guy or anything like that. I can barely touch my shins without bending my knees. I thought I'd look like a total moron with these strangers, standing on the side of a grassy hill, lifting our hands in the sky, then bringing them back to our chest saying things like, "I take in ALL of the beauty . . ."

But then we started doing it. At first, I would peek over at the other participants to see if they were laughing at me, but everyone was fully engaged. I became less self-conscious and started trying to engage my heart in the movements of our bodies. The foolishness of it somehow became part of its healing in me. It was the letting down of guards, the letting go of fear and self-consciousness. (Isn't this the effect that worship should have on a human being?) I stood with these strange people doing these strange movements, yet somehow there was no shame. We didn't know anything about each other, but we were sharing this moment together in silent presence. We kneeled in the grass, imagining ourselves in the river of God, fully seen, fully known, fully loved, and my tears fell to the grass like falling shackles.

After a few days of this, I began to experience everything in greater capacity. God felt close. The world brimmed with life. I had time to really taste the pasta that I cooked. I went into town a couple of times to see some of the sites and history that is so rich in Assisi. Normally, in going to an old cathedral, I would look around for the highlights.

Anybody famous do anything in here?

Anything I should take a quick picture of before I get out of here?

This time was different. I could just sit there and stare at a single piece of artwork for a half an hour. And it wasn't that I was empty-headed or slow of thought. It was that I was so aware of life bursting through everything. I saw things in a statue that I never would normally notice. It was as though God was speaking through every piece of art and architecture around me. Every color was richer and every sound more beautiful. I was present and aware, and the joy I experienced in Assisi was some of the most profound of my life.

After a few days, an interesting thing happened. In burnout, I had been extremely unproductive as an artist. Anything that I tried to create felt forced and uninspired. Trying to write felt like scratching the bottom of a barrel, with fragments of wood splintering underneath my fingernails. When I was in Assisi with my lungs full of breath, there came a point where I couldn't do anything but exhale. I remember sitting there so full of life and feeling like I just needed to express it. So I sat down and wrote a piece for a string quartet. But it wasn't art created out of burden or obligation. It was the only appropriate response to the life building in my chest. Work wasn't toil, but simply the act of exhaling. It was the natural expression of my humanity.

In Assisi, hope was restored. The world was worth ordering. Music was worth writing.

This is what hope does. It allows us to believe that our work matters. Even if nobody seems to care about it. Even if the crowd takes no notice of you or your work. Hope allows us to approach the seeming insignificance of our work with inspiration and perspective. Hope allows a single grain of salt to recognize that it is part of a meal.

Jesus talked a lot about little things. Things like seeds and yeast and pennies. The entire story of Jesus is drenched with the idea of God being found in small and insignificant things. Even at the climax of the story—Jesus' resurrection—it's such a small splash at first. Jesus didn't suddenly appear on the temple steps in a blinding flash of light. No trumpets sounded from heaven as Jesus marched into Rome. He appeared to some women. Then he went and ate with his friends. Then he left, and his friends sat in little rooms and prayed and broke bread together. It was all so small. Like seeds and yeast and pennies.

In the silence of Assisi, I found hope. I began becoming more comfortable with who I was made to be as a creator. Finding a home within my own skin and even within my own industry. Recognizing that even within an industry that has a lot of flaws, there is a lot of beauty to be found.

The Practice of Hope

Hope pulls us towards the light, towards the waterfall. It is not something that you can force, but it is something that you can find.

This is why people have long turned to practices like solitude, prayer, study, and meditation. These disciplines help us find our breath; they help us become more human. They help us hear the Voice.

Of course, you don't have to travel all the way to Assisi to practice these disciplines. You can get a good start by just slowing down and limiting stimulation now and then. Hope needs space to grow. Try turning down the noise for a period of time. Turn off the TV. Sit in front of a fire and listen to a record instead, or just sit there. Watch the flames bend and writhe over the darkening wood. Listen to the crackle of escaping vapors; look deeply at the subtle changing colors of the ash and embers.

Practice being fully present with something. Perhaps you may find something of God there. Go outside and look at the stars. Not for just a few seconds—lay a blanket in the yard, lie on your back and really look at the stars. Try to let your heart feel the incomprehensible size and grandeur of the universe. Take the time to really attend to a meal, a good book, a piece of music, or a sunrise. The point is to be fully present, to not be swept up into the distraction of a thousand voices, but to learn how to simply and fully attend to one. Then, when one enters back into the noisy world that we live in, even the million colors together are more vibrant because you have learned to better see color in its essence. To truly see is to find hope.

14. LOVE: THESE GLOVES

Remember that youth conference with the countdowns and pyrotechnics? We ended up being a sort of house band for that conference as it toured across the nation. It was a great opportunity for us as a struggling new band. We were suddenly playing in front of thousands of new people every weekend.

Plus, we were enjoying it. Even though the conference was more conservative than I am, we had some meaningful spiritual experiences worshiping with those kids. We were making some great friends as a result of being part of this organization. We were making connections with influential people in that market, which translates to more gigs, more influence, and so on.

But then something happened. We were asked to be a part of one of the teaching sessions. They wanted us to play music behind the teacher during key moments of his talk. They sent us a video of the session so we could learn the music and come prepared to the event. On the video, a band was set up on the huge stage behind the speaker. They played cover songs as the preacher paced back and forth, energizing the room. It all felt pretty corny, but I tried to stay open-minded as I watched because I really wanted to be helpful to them if I could.

But then the teacher started talking about gay people. He began to warn the kids about the gay *agenda* and how *the homosexuals* are scheming to influence this generation. Here is an excerpt from an email that he sent me later:

> I guarantee there are teens in the crowd in Iowa that have been tricked and deceived by what the gay activists have "taught" them. They are confused right now in their sexual identity. I cannot leave them there without hope in the name of "loving" those that deceived them.

Now, maybe I'm just ignorant or naïve, but I have no idea who these elusive, gay tricksters are. Perhaps there are dark rooms in the underbelly of Hollywood high-rises with sinister-looking lesbians laughing maniacally and plotting world domination, but I've never heard of them. Regardless, there was something about this teaching that made me feel queasy.

At one point, the band on the video started playing the Village People's "YMCA," and the crowd stood to their feet, laughing and doing the hand motions. It felt very much like mockery to me.

I had a decision to make.

Keep the gig along with the money, influence, and relationships that it provided. Or make some sort of moral stand and probably lose the gig and all of the aforementioned gig bounty.

Up to this point in the book, the discussion of creativity has been primarily focused on the internal world of the creator. But, of course, how we order creation has other and more important ramifications than the artist's own artistic integrity or satisfaction. The ways in which we order creation are the ways in which the world takes its shape.

Most human work adds value to the world, making it a better place. But some work doesn't.

Just because something is creative, lucrative, or practical doesn't mean it is worth doing. Faith, doubt, and hope are the stuff of good soil for creating and cultivating, as are honesty, integrity, patience, courage and any number of nutrients. But all of these only find their true value when they are made consummate in love.

There is no richer soil than love. It's the end of the rabbit hole. Without love, all else is meaningless. Love creates. Without love, there is no reason to create. Love is what holds a family, a society, and a humanity together. And if St. Paul is right, love is the magnet that pulls everything in and holds the entire universe together (Colossians 1:17).

Everything beautiful grows from love. Conversely, every broken and twisted thing comes from fear—the opposite of love. For the creator, love should be the ultimate standard and aspiration for the work. Fear, on the other hand, should never be relied on in making our creative decisions. Fear will never lead us down the right path. In the end, fear only leads to a sullying of the good, a perversion of the beautiful.

Fear is what drives bigotry. I have a hard time believing that it was love for gay people that was driving the youth conference to ask the band to play "YMCA" to the laughter and jeering of thousands of teenagers.

I'm embarrassed to say that there was a day when I would not have noticed nor cared very much about the bigotry of the youth conference teaching. I remember with a pit in my stomach the day when the teenaged Lisa and

168 \\ MICHAEL GUNGOR

I visited Dallas while we were dating. Since both of us had grown up in very conservative environments in very small towns, we didn't know a lot of gay people.

So there we were, teenage fundamentalists driving around Dallas looking for a place to eat. We found a little neighborhood that looked like it had several little cafés and shops. We parked the car and started walking, but after a few blocks, I suddenly noticed all of the rainbow flags. I squeezed Lisa's hand and looked with horror at several same sex couples walking down the sidewalk. I whispered as though we had found ourselves on a strange planet full of man-eating aliens: "Lisa, this is the *gay* neighborhood. Let's get out of here!" And we literally ran away.

We told our friends about it and everyone laughed. Not at us, but with us.

To our gay friends now: We are sorry. It's really humiliating to even tell this story. But the crazy thing about it is that we didn't actually harbor personal hatred toward gay people. And though it doesn't excuse our behavior, we were products of systemic bigotry. Like a white child in the 1950s who was taught that "colored's" have their place in society because they had been cursed by God, our bigotry was handed down to us, and we couldn't see it yet.

But through the years, grace found its way into our vision and began to break our small-minded bigotry apart.

Grace in Auschwitz

Several years ago, Lisa and I had the chance to spend a month in Europe. My dad had been invited to the Vatican to be a part of an ecumenical dialogue around Christmas time, and being a generous man, he decided to bring the family with him. Lisa and I decided to make good use of the free tickets to Europe and stay for a while. We bought a train pass and headed though Rome, Florence, and Venice, then continued on to Vienna and Salzburg, then up through the Czech Republic into Poland.

The winter was starting to set in, and while the thought of continuing to head north wasn't entirely appealing, we both wanted to visit Auschwitz.

I know this may seem macabre. When most couples go to Europe for a Christmas vacation, they probably would rather spend their time in places like Paris or Amsterdam, or really any place that isn't the site of horrendous mass murder. But for some reason, of all the beautiful and romantic places to visit in Europe, we wanted to go to one of the darkest places on the planet—the Nazi death camp at Auschwitz.

I think I wanted to go there because most of the time, I felt so insulated in America. As Americans, we live in this little protected bubble of homeland security, landscaped sidewalks, and alarmed cars with plenty of cup-holders. I wanted my world to open up. I learned about things like wars and concentration camps in school, but it felt so distant and abstract. I wanted to feel the unspeakable tragedy of something like the Holocaust as more than a historical statistic. I had read Holocaust survivor Elie Wiesel's account of his experience at Auschwitz, and he had written, "To forget the dead would be akin to killing them a second time." I knew there was something important about trying to feel the weight of what happened in Poland in the 1940s.

So as our train rattled through the Polish snow-laden forests in the middle of the night, I stared out the window into the fog and tried to imagine the Poland of six or seven decades ago. I imagined that it wouldn't have looked all that different. Then, when we got off the train in Krakow and checked into our hotel, I thought about how the neighborhood where I was getting into my warm hotel bed had held Jewish inhabitants who were so suddenly and violently torn away from their homes and imprisoned in the ghettos. I wondered what it must have been like to live in a nation that had suffered the loss of over twenty percent of its population as a result of the relentless brutality of the Nazis.

First thing in the morning, we took a train to Oswiecim, which is the town nearest to the death camps. As we walked through the town toward the camps, I saw an old Polish woman wearing a puffy blue coat. She was slightly hunched over, walking into the freezing wind. I watched her for a little while, and suddenly everything started sinking in.

She was probably here, I thought. *She was probably a little girl.*

These were *real people.* This is a *real* camp outside of a *real* town with *real* people. People like me. People who knew that it was wrong, but were afraid. Real people who saw the trains come in packed with other real people. This little old lady may have smelled the smoke of the crematoriums.

As we entered the iron gates of the camp, the thought that kept shuddering through my soul was: *This actually happened.*

This actually happened . . . as I stood silently at the flower-lined execution wall where countless moms and dads, brothers and sisters were lined up and shot—not in grainy black and white like in the documentaries, but in vivid, gory color. The cold blues of winter sky and Nazi eyes. The reds of blood and swastika, the white of snow. The saltiness of tears. The inescapable physicality of it all screamed at me from the room stacked with dilapidated child-sized shoes, and tore at my heart from the massive, dark grey tangle of human hair that the Nazis had cut from the heads of best friends and lovers, musicians and bankers, pet-owners and joke-tellers.

These confiscated pocket-watches belonged to real men. Men like my dad. These baby toys belonged to real babies. We hadn't had Amélie yet, and if we had, I don't know how I would have kept any semblance of composure. Amélie has baby dolls. They make her laugh and squeal with delight. What kind of evil does it take to do the things that they did to people's baby girls? Violently pulling babies from their daddy's arms. Killing them. I felt the echo of the realest and darkest kind of evil in those rooms.

Every Jew, Christian, gay person, gypsy, or prisoner of war that was dragged into that damned place was a human being who experienced love and fear, who laughed and cried. Who stretched her arms to the sky when she yawned, just like the rest of us. Who dreamed of the people he loved when he went to sleep at night, just like the rest of us. It was too much.

The tears welled in my eyes as I was hammered with the reality that every person that was stripped, shaved and thrown into the gas chambers was somebody's baby, somebody's lover, somebody's friend, and every single one of them was God's beloved creation. Fearfully and wonderfully made. And it was real people like me, with hands and feet, thoughts and conscience—men with families of their own who knew what they were doing and who pushed the button to release the gas.

How could this have actually happened?

The tears fell.

The tears that ran down my cheeks were certainly not the first, nor the last, that would be shed in that place.

After we left that abominable camp, I tried to imagine how a human mind could fall prey to such darkness. What would it take for someone to commit atrocities like this? How do you rid yourself of compassion for your fellow human beings to the point where you can slam babies against walls and throw grandmothers into gas chambers?

The only thing I could imagine is that you would have to really believe that the people you are doing this to aren't human in the same way that you are. Surely these Nazis had to separate themselves from the people that they were killing. This wasn't just a few psychopaths. There were millions of people involved in or at least overlooking what was happening in Europe to the Jewish people. Soldiers. Politicians. Neighbors. Policemen. Co-workers. Family friends. Nearly everyone. The Jews were seen as something less than human. For this to happen, there would have to be such a significant separation between the "us" that the Germans wanted to build and the "them" that stood in the way.

Us. Them. This is at the heart of evil in the world. This is what allows holocausts to happen.

So when I was asked by this very large and very influential Christian ministry to play music behind a teacher spouting propaganda about how *those* homosexuals are scheming against *us*, perhaps you can understand some of my apprehension. The kind of "Christianity" that gathers into arenas to make fun of gay people is not the kind of religion that I want to have anything to do with. That's not the kind of art I want to create. I saw the end result of racial, religious, and sexual bigotry within the barbed wire of Auschwitz; so, no I will not play your song.

Everything Grows from Love

> *Dear friends, let us love one another, for love is of God. Everyone who loves is born of God and knows God. Whoever does not love does not know God, because God is love.*
> *1 John 4:7-8*

According to 1 John, love is the measuring stick of how much someone knows God. Not head knowledge. Not accurate theology. Not faith. Not how much Scripture one has memorized or how many good deeds one has racked up. Love.

This is radically controversial because if it is true, then it is possible for someone who knows absolutely nothing about theology to know God better than the "experts"—the pastors, priests, or those with Ph.D.'s in theology. I have spent a lot of time reading books, philosophizing and studying doctrines of God, but according to 1 John, that doesn't necessarily have any correlation to actually knowing God.

God is love.

Love is not something that is most clearly understood by analysis or rationalization. In fact, love seems to transcend our reasoning. Love is better experienced than understood.

I saw this documentary the other day that was about the church in America. As always with such films, this documentary showed plenty for those of us inside the walls of Sunday morning to be embarrassed about, but there was this part at the end that really moved me.

It showed a group of Christians in Portland, Oregon, who have a thriving ministry to the homeless in the city. These Jesus followers go and do as their Lord instructed them to do. They feed people, clothe people, and sometimes even literally wash their feet.

The film cuts to a lady on her knees as she scrubs the filthy feet of a man who looks like he hasn't bathed in awhile. She is wearing the required rubber gloves to protect her from disease, but you can see that her work is not a chore to her. It is an act of love.

A couple minutes later, the interviewer asks her what the hardest part about doing something like this is. We might expect her to say it's the time away from family or the hard, dirty work of cleaning filthy people all night. Instead, she pauses, and her eyes well with tears.

"I hate that we have to wear these gloves."

God is love.

Any doctrine that is unfounded in this love is completely worthless. Any Christian theology that leads to human division, isolation, or elitism has missed the point. Any knowledge without love, in the words of St. Paul, is nothing.

The closing remark in the email from the prominent evangelical Christian leader of that youth conference was, "Yes, we must love AND we must speak truth." In his mind, love and truth seem to somehow be in tension. It's as if love is the buttering up of an individual before you can get to the truth. Such is the clever gimmick of fundamentalism. But it's not love.

Love is not a prelude to the truth or a less offensive style of delivering the truth. It is the deepest truth.

If love dictates that we should communicate things that are hard to hear sometimes, than that is what we should do. But that does not separate truth and love. They should be one and the same.

I believe that the story of Jesus is the most fertile creative ground possible because for the artist, love becomes a soil with infinite nourishment for newness. This communal soil has so much more potential than the cold, dead individualistic survivalism that our culture has to offer. As an artist, I want to write music that tries to tap into this soil even if I have to carry some sort of stigma or label as a result. If I choose love, I know there will probably be more gigs and opportunities like the youth conference that I will lose. Love may cost you everything, but it is the only thing worth anything.

Creator, choose love.

Love creates. Fear un-creates. I know this because I used to live in a religion based in fear.

I used to get on Internet chat rooms and argue against the evolutionists because if they were right, then Adam and Eve weren't naked people in a garden six thousand years ago. And if the Adam and Eve story wasn't literally true, how could I know that Jesus rose from the dead? I argued with such fervor, trying to keep every link in my religious chains sturdy. That's why I ran away from the gay people in Dallas. Fear, and not love, was at the core of my faith. I was an idolater. I worshiped my Christianity more than Christ. I worshiped my beliefs and ideas of God rather than using my beliefs as a diving board into the community and love of God. This fear didn't propel me into the world as a creator, as salt and light; it separated me from the world. It limited my creativity. It imprisoned me.

I've tasted fear, and I've tasted love. As for me and my art, I choose love. I choose love in the hope that it is love that has chosen me.

CONCLUSION: LET THERE BE

Normally, when you set out to make an album, you have to have to take all sorts of marketing questions into account. Questions like, "Which song is the radio single?" Or, in the my particular segment of the music world, "Which songs will be accessible for churches?"

For years, those questions mattered to me. I had entered competitions, recorded albums, and tried to schmooze with people that could help me advance in my musical career. But after failing miserably to succeed over and over again, I kind of lost hope. After years of trying to "make it", I finally gave up. I let go of what Becky[1] (the name that Christian radio stations have given to their target demographic) or the marketers, promoters, label, management, or anyone else thought of the music. In the ashes of my big musical aspirations, I was left with a simple desire to create some meaningful art that was consonant with my soul. I just wanted to make some good, honest music, not as an attempt to become rich or famous but as a way of sincerely reflecting my faith, doubt, hope and love into the creation around me.

So when my band had a new album due to our label, I decided to start making aesthetic decisions that lined up more appropriately with my soul. I started trusting the passion and love in my gut rather than the nagging, fearful questions at the back of my mind.

For instance, at the time, my band was called "The Michael Gungor Band." For some reason, that name just didn't feel right anymore. It felt sort of generic or something—kind of like my career had become. The fearful nagging reminded me that we would lose market recognition (and therefore comfort and security) by changing the band name, but the aesthetic just really didn't align with my vision for the kind of art I wanted to create. So we tried chopping off "The", "Michael", and "Band"—leaving

1   For more info on Becky, see Appendix 2.

my odd and ambiguous-sounding last name "Gungor." That felt better. Even though it was still my last name, the ambiguity felt freeing somehow. Like the art could take center stage rather than me.

In deciding how to record the new album, I wanted to find a way to listen to the right voices. I didn't want to get caught up into industry noise or everyone else's opinion of the art we were creating. So rather than hiring a proper studio where industry people could stop by and listen to what we were doing, we rented a house in the mountains where we didn't even have cell phone service.

We hauled some gear up there and put together a makeshift studio. Lisa would make us breakfast in the morning. We'd start a fire. We'd make music. We'd go to sleep. It was beautiful. Up there, the world was so quiet that we could hear what we needed to hear.

There was a communal aspect to all of this that made the creation of the art all the more meaningful. The creation of art can tend to become a hyper-individualistic endeavor. What happened up in the mountains, though, is that we had all of these people who were willing to listen to the voices inside of them and create something meaningful. Something beautiful started emerging. A conversation between these voices that sounded less like the voice of the crowd and more like the voice of a community. The voice of a community can be one of the most beautiful voices possible.[2] It is not a trumping of the individual voice, but rather a harmonization of individual voices. It's still truthful, but it is bigger than you.

At first, nothing much happened with the album commercially. For the first several months, nobody paid much attention to it. But I was ok with it because, for me, that album became sacred music in the truest sense of the word—not because of some sort of genre classification[3] or religious

---

2 Christian theology would say that the voice of God is the voice of a community. I like that.

3 See Appendix 2 if you are interested in my ideas about genre. In early drafts of the book, I actually had included that section within the flow of the book. But it just seemed a bit more specific to my own industry than the rest of the book is, so I threw it in the back as a bonus for any who might be interested to hear more about my industry.

content within the lyrics, but because we created the art with open hands. It was an offering. For me, it was the interplay of dust with the divine, the image of a communal God imprinting itself onto creation.

I also turned my attention to the kinds of gigs we were spending our time and energy on. Up to that point, we had simply played at the places that invited us and could afford us. Conferences, big churches, and the like. We had become a kind of a plug-and-play artist that formed our creative expression to fit whatever situation we were in.

You need some high-energy music to get the teenagers at your conference hyped up? Sure! That will be $3,000.

You want to hire a band to lead a hymn sing for the elderly people at your Baptist Church? Sure! That will be $3,000.

I don't think there was anything inherently wrong with that. Youth conferences and old Baptist churches sometimes need musicians, and musicians sometimes need youth conferences and old Baptist churches. But in the process of working, I had somehow stopped listening to that Voice that inspired me to work in the first place. My job had become a job rather than a calling.

So, I decided to put on a series of concerts that we would call "Beautiful Things Events." I wanted to create the kind of space that more intentionally matched the spirit of the music and what was happening in our souls as we wrote and recorded it. So we rented out some little clubs and theatres, found some orchestral musicians, and composed a three-movement piece that incorporated music, film, and poetry, and was different than anything I had ever seen or done before.

The events were expensive. I lost a lot of money doing them. But people really enjoyed them. We started getting requests around the country to do more of them. They started selling out. People started telling their friends about our music, and things really started changing for us.

The ironic thing about all of this was that my art really started connecting with people as soon as I stopped trying please everyone. The album ended up being nominated for Grammy awards. We heard from critics and crowd alike how the music would speak to them. I was glad that a lot of people seemed to like it, but I also couldn't help but smile at the irony.

Here is a paradox for the creator: if you love your work, let it go.[4] Because if you grip it too tightly, you will strangle it. If you hold it in open hands, you may actually find that the work has a life of its own. Creativity is more about listening and following than it is about forcing or manipulating. The truth for the creator is that you have a very limited control over anything in the world, even your own creation. You can work on it. You can help mold and shape its form. But there will come a point in the creative process where your creation is what it is. There comes a point where there is nothing left to do but to rest. To open your hands and let it go. You cannot control how others will receive it. They will see it as they see it and use it however they want to use it. Your creativity is a gift. Your work is a gift. Your life is a gift. Enjoy it. Love it. Do the work, but then let it go. Let it be.

Let There Be

What makes the tree continue to grow toward the sky? What drives the cells to give themselves fully to your body's creation and function? What holds the atoms together? If life is evolving, what is the pull that keeps life fighting to live, to reproduce? There is something. Something that keeps pulling. Drawing us like a magnet toward becoming.

God.

Perhaps God is not an old man in the sky but that which draws the sky to open up into reality. If God is infinite and Trinitarian and shall be all in all like the Christians have said for 2000 years, then perhaps some of our perennial questions —"Why does God allow . . .?"—assume a juvenile view of God. Perhaps God is not the puppet master of the universe, but

---

4   Matthew 16:25

the future toward which the universe opens. Perhaps God is not the single subject watchmaker of the past that wound up the universe and let it play out on its own, but instead is the Reality of the future into which all things live and move and come into being.

If this is true, then God is the ground of art. For from Him and through Him and to Him are all things (Romans 11:36).

Art is the ordering of the becoming creation. It is the divine image within every human being—the joining of the Voice that sang, sings, and will sing "Let there be" and there was, there is, and there shall be.

Art is the imprint of our humanity on the created order—the echo of the divine image etched into the husks of trees and curvatures of electricity and light. It is our shadow cast upon the earth, our names scrawled in the wet cement of the universe, and even though the temporality of life ensures that the waves of time will wash clean the sand of all our castles, there is something within the human spirit that demands the effort. Our art is divine breath once again breathed into dust, and it is air worth breathing.

For me, this is the ledge of the canyon. This is the scenic overlook of why human beings create—the ground from which I can imagine and plant. My hope in writing this book is to show you what I have seen. This canyon is vast, and there is infinite work waiting to be done down in its valleys.

So to the artist, to the creator, I ask: How will you respond? How will you create?

Will you listen to the voice of your critics in determining what sort of art you should make? Will you listen to the voices within your culture—the demand for commercial viability, the pull towards the lowest common denominator? Will you listen to the voice of the numb that complains that it's not fast enough, bright enough, sexy enough? Or will you listen to the voice that speaks from your very cells—the voice that always is saying, "Let there be"?

Will you be courageous enough to create the art that you truly desire to create rather than settling for the art that you feel is necessary?

It is a dangerous place—that place where you purposefully lift your head into the abyss of the unknown and let your voice harmonize with the constantly singing voice of the Creator. This place of creation is always riddled with risk. The ego trembles in knowledge of the countless eyes about to stare into your work—eyes of judgment, eagerness, jealousy, ridicule or joy. Creating is risky, and it can be painful.

This is part of why the artist must be rooted in love. Love can move you through the pain. Fear will only make you avoid it.

It is in this precarious and sacred space that all great human accomplishment is created. To live in this space is dangerous, but it is exhilarating. It is freedom. It is life embraced with full arms and chest.

Our faith and intention determines whether the genius and power of this godlike ability to rule over creation—forming it, molding it however we wish—is used for good or evil. Some people fashion stone and earth into iPhones or love letters; others form the same basic materials into swords and atomic bombs. Whether or not we create is not up to us. We are human, and creating is what we do. Every interaction, movement, and decision is creativity at work. We are all artists. We all order creation around us into the world that we want to make. All work speaks from something and to something. But what our work speaks to, what we create—that much is left in our hands.

Will you create in a way that brings beauty into the world? Or ugliness? Life or death? Heaven or hell?

Because when you've chosen your soil, the planting can finally begin. The artist must come to a place where she moves beyond the philosophies and mysticality of art and into the craft of it. Steven Pressfield writes of the artist in *The War of Art*, "She understands that all creative endeavor is holy, but she doesn't dwell on it. She knows if she thinks about that too much, it will paralyze her. So she concentrates on technique."

This book has been a reminder that our art is holy. The proper response to such an idea is not to let these ideas stay on the level of theory. That would be like a man reminding himself of his love for his wife only so he could sit around and read romance novels all day. His remembrance ought to lead him to her physical embrace.

The philosophy of romantic love is best expressed in longing glances and kisses. The philosophy of art is best expressed with paint on your face and dirt under your fingernails.

A Benediction

May you, son, daughter, image of the very Creator God, fearfully and wonderfully made, knit together in your mother's womb, fully seen, fully known, and fully loved, see with eyes that are open wide. Hear the Voice that speaks from inside of you with ears attuned and mind unshackled. Taste and see the goodness of the One who shall be all and in all.

May your heart be opened to the love that formed you and everything else, the love that holds all things together and shall make all things new in the end, and may that love that was broken and poured out for you impel you into the world to break your own self open to be poured out for the world that God so loves. Poured out in acts of justice and mercy, poured out in good and hard work that brings order rather than disorder. Poured out in songs and liturgies, business plans and water colors, child-rearing and policy-making.

May your life be a brush in the very hand of God—painting new creation into every nook and cranny of reality that your shadow graces. Be courageous. Be free. Prune that which needs pruning, and water that which thirsts for righteousness.

You are the body of Christ, the light of the world. Pick up your hammer. Your brush. Your trumpet. Your skillet. Your pen. Lift up your head. And walk. Run. Dance. Fly. The great Artist, the future God, calls you into being. So go into your world, your valley, your garden, and create with His grace and in His peace.

Amen.

Appendix 1:

A Snapshot of American Pop

You know how most of what you buy at the grocery store has a nutrition label detailing a food's calories, fat, sugar, and so on? Consider this appendix a nutrition label for American pop music. What are we consuming in our typical musical diet today?

At the time of this writing, these were the top ten purchased songs in the United States:

1. We Found Love – Rihanna
2. It Will Rain – Bruno Mars
3. Sexy & I Know It – LMFAO[1]
4. Good Feeling – Flo Rida
5. The One that Got Away – Katy Perry
6. Someone Like You – Adele
7. Moves Like Jagger – Maroon 5 featuring Christina Aguilera
8. Without You – David Guetta featuring Usher
9. Paradise – Coldplay
10. 5 O'Clock – T-Pain featuring Wiz Khalifa & Lily Allen

These songs are remarkably similar. This is not an eclectic mix of music. You will not find a country song here, an indie rock song there, a hardcore song, and then a couple of pop songs. They are all pop songs, but even that might be too broad a label for them. These songs fit into a very specific formula of current "hits." Let's look at their raw musical facts.

---

1   I realize that earlier in the book, I said that this song was number one. It was. The appendix and that chapter were written in different weeks.

Here are the tempos (beats per minute) of these songs:

1. 128 (Rihanna)
2. 75 (Bruno Mars)
3. 130 (LMFAO)
4. 128 (Flo Rida)
5. 134 (Katy Perry)
6. 132 (Adele)
7. 128 (Maroon 5)
8. 128 (David Guetta)
9. 70 (Coldplay)
10. 84 (T-Pain)

These tempos are extremely close, too close to be random. Normal song tempos range from very slow ballads that can be 50–60BPM to fast bebop or punk tunes that may be as fast as 300BPM. The hits today do not vary nearly this much. Look at the tempos of these songs on this graph:

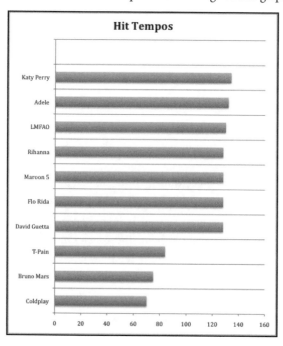

As you can see, these songs tend to gravitate around two approximate tempo marks. One is the mid-120–130 mark. Four of the top ten songs are at the head-bobbing tempo of 128. That's the pace of an energetic walk and an easy tempo to dance to. It feels "up," but not frenetic.

The other tempo center is around the mid-70s. This is an emotional, or "groove," tempo. It's sexy. It's not sleepy, but it can feel more relaxed.

The average tempo for pop songs has increased in the last several years. The average BPM of these songs is around 113. The average BPM of the top ten songs of 1997 was around 97. The primary center of tempo gravity for songs in the late 90s seemed to be about 20 BPM slower than now, often close to 100-110. Think of Britney Spears' "Hit Me Baby One More Time," Dave Matthew Band's "Crash Into Me," Backstreet Boy's "Everybody," The Wallflower's "One Headlight," Lauryn Hill's "Doo Wop," and so on. Formulas change over time.

Nearly every one of the choruses of these songs is built around four chords. Often these four chords repeat over the entire song, as synthesizers are used to fill the primary musical space in a rhythmic pattern that we hear over and over again.

Interestingly, within the chord structures of the songs, major and minor chords are fairly balanced, so that you normally don't hear more than two majors or minors in a row. If you don't know music theory, here is a key to at least explain which chord numbers are major and minor:

1: major
2: minor
3: minor
4: major
5: major
6: minor

Now, with that in mind, check out the primary chord patterns over the choruses in these top ten songs:

1. We Found Love – 6, 4, 1, 2 (minor, major, major, minor)
2. It Will Rain – 4, 5, 3, 6 (major, major, minor, minor)
3. Sexy & I Know It – (this one actually only has one minor chord)
4. Good Feeling – 6, 1, 5, 4 (minor, major, major, major)
5. The One that Got Away – 1, 3, 6, 4 (major, minor, minor, major)
6. Someone Like You – 1, 5, 6, 4 (major, major, minor, major)
7. Moves Like Jagger – 6, 2, 4 (minor, minor, major)
8. Without You – 1, 4, 6, 4 (major, major, minor, major)
9. Paradise – 2, 4, 1, 5, 5/7 (minor, major, major, major, but 5/7 is an inversion of a major chord that makes it sound a bit more minor)
10. 5 O'Clock – 1, 3, b7, 4 (major, minor, major, but the only chord in the top 10 outside of the diatonic major scale, major)

As you can see, the further down the list we go, the farther away it seems to get from the purest form of the formula, which is four repeating synth chords, of which two are major and two are minor. This applies to the length of the song as well. While all of these songs are within the three-to-five minute range, the top songs are slightly shorter in duration than the ones toward the bottom of the list.

Lyrically, nearly every one of these songs is about some sort of relational, sexual angst. Breakups, love in the midst of trouble, love unrequited, etc. There are exceptions to this, though—LMFAO changes things up by singing ironically about how sexy they are.

This formula does not contain all of the criteria for making a song a hit, but, clearly, there is a formula. Such is our culture's musical diet right now.

Appendix 2:

Christian Pizza

A typical conversation I might have on an airplane:

Stranger (*upon seeing the guitar on my back*): Hey, are you gonna play us something?

Michael: Ha ha! Maybe, we'll see! (*Note to jokesters: anybody who regularly carries a guitar onto a plane is tired of this joke.*)

Stranger: You know, I'm not sure that guitar is going to fit in the overhead . . .

Michael (*trying to stay nice*): Yeah, it does actually.

I place the guitar in the overhead bin and close it without a problem. I realize my seat is right next to the stranger and sit down.

Stranger: So, what kind of music do you play?

It is here that I have a difficult time knowing how to answer.

If you asked Bill iTunes or John Google this question about Michael Gungor, the answer that you would find would be "Christian and Gospel." There are a number of reasons that this is not the answer I would prefer to give someone, especially a stranger on a plane. It is not because I am embarrassed about the spiritual content of our music. I'm not. It's essentially a language problem.

It actually gets kind of complicated. So to begin, let's take another jaunt back to my fundamentalist days.

Here's how art worked in the religious subculture that I grew up in: If you want to be a painter, and you want God to be happy with your art, you better paint crosses or doves flying around a globe or something. If you want to be a singer, and you want to use your gift for God, you need to sing Christian music. The more JPM's (Jesus' Per Minute), the better.

I loved music. I loved God. So I tried to write Christian music. I wasn't great at it.

I lost my first Christian music competition when I was eighteen. It was a big seminar held in the Rocky Mountains where the winners could win things like Christian record deals.

In the first category, instrumental music, my toughest competition was a blind guitarist. I didn't know how to feel about that. He was a really good player, and I felt bad for him because he was blind and all; but man, there was still a big part of me that wanted to crush that visually impaired acoustic shredder into the ground. No luck there, though. I came in second. I hoped for better luck in the songwriting part of the competition.

I had submitted a song called "What a God" that was a big hit at my church. People would actually start chanting "WHAT A GOD! WHAT A GOD!" at the end of services. This would happen quite regularly. I think it may have had something to do with all of the solos in it. Acoustic guitar solos, sax solos, percussion solos, drums solos . . . it was the late 90s, and people ate solos for breakfast.

The judges told me that the song was trite.

Trite.

Stupid judges. They must not have heard the incredible solos.

In retrospect, the song *was* trite, but I still felt like I had been robbed, so I came back the next year. This time, I had written a song in a minor key with a 7/8 time signature, and I thought it was pretty amazing. I was confident that the judges would think so as well. They did not. They told me that odd time signatures do not work well in Christian music. They told me that people like Sting might be able to get away with it, but he is not in Christian music.

I tried for a long time to be part of the Christian music industry. I even went to the Dove Awards one time.[1] I sat there in my nice suit, daydreaming about what it would be like to win one of those someday.

So, yeah, there would have been a day that I would have gladly told the stranger on the plane that I played Christian music. But in the years of trying to make it in the Christian music industry, I came to discover how fundamentally fraught with peril an idea like Christian music can be.

First, and least importantly, there is the problem of the idea of genre. This is my first hurdle with the stranger on the plane. He's asking for a genre, and so much about the idea of genres drives me crazy. Genres are all about labeling, marketing, and boxing art into imaginary constructs for the purpose of making money.

Genres are arbitrary. You can't accurately classify art into categories like you can with lizards or different species of ferns. In science, classification works well—"It's got four limbs, some hair, milk for its babies, lungs, and warm blood. It's a mammal." In art, the situation is not so cut and dry.

How many jokes must be included in a screenplay before the drama becomes a comedy? How many bombs must explode before the thriller becomes an action movie? If a rock band decides to start using banjos rather than electric guitars, are they still a rock band, or have they suddenly become a country or bluegrass band?

---

1 The Dove Awards are the Christian version of the Grammy's.

If musical genres were based on concrete and consistent musical characteristics, the marketers would have to create new genres in the record stores for every new, innovative artist that comes along. That's not what happens. What happens is that the marketers simply categorize the artist's album into the alternative section or the pop section or wherever they think it will have the best chance of selling. A genre is an imagined box that marketers have found to be effective as a marketing channel to a certain type of consumer.

What, for instance, does a typical country music fan look like in your imagination? What is he wearing? How does he speak? Ok, now think of a typical hip-hop fan. Same questions. How do you imagine him?

I doubt that you are imagining both the country fan and the hip-hop fan to be two identical middle-aged Asian businessmen in suits with no discernable differences between them or their lifestyles other than what is playing on their iPods.

Both country music and hip-hop music come out of a certain type of culture. Country music originated in southern parts of the United States in the 1920s. This was the same culture that had given birth to the concept of the cowboy. Country stars often wear cowboy clothing, which is clothing designed to help a person do the job of a cowboy, not sing music on a stage. A cowboy hat is intended to help keep a rancher protected from the weather. Cowboy boots were designed to help protect a cowboy while he rides his horse.

Most country artists aren't riding horses to and from the stage. That's not why country singers wear this clothing. Country music is perceived to come out of a certain lifestyle. That lifestyle has all of its own boundary markers that separate it from other cultures and lifestyles. Country artists wear cowboy hats as social boundary markers for their particular subculture.

The same is true for hip-hop. Hip-hop came out of the lifestyle of poor or working class people living in crowded urban centers. Hip-hop and rap often address issues that are familiar to their urban source—economic pressures, crime, drugs, gangs, violence, and so on. What is odd is that most successful rappers or hip-hop artists do not live in "the hood" anymore. They live in the rich areas. The style of sagging pants that many of these artists wear is believed to have originated in the prisons where belts were not allowed for the fear that the inmates might hang themselves with them. These artists are not in prison, and most of them probably never have been, but crime and a perceived oppression from authority figures is part of the subculture that gives birth to the art, so they've come to sag their pants.

So all of this is my first problem with answering the stranger's question— he's asking for a genre, and I don't want to jump into any of his boxes.

The second reason I am not comfortable telling the stranger that I make "Christian music" is because I believe that this sort of categorization is precisely the kind of destructive separation of the sacred and the secular that is the result of fundamentalism, idolatry, and remnants of Gnosticism.[2] That sort of division between sacred and profane makes for a small and anemic faith that is only relevant to the tiny corners of existence that we allow it to inhabit.

In *Velvet Elvis*, Rob Bell writes, "'Christian is a great noun and a poor adjective." I agree with him. When the word "Christian" is used as an adjective, the assumption is that the essence of Christianity is something that can be transferred to a lifeless object. If Christianity is simply a set of lifeless dogmas and ideas, then one can certainly copy and paste those ideas onto any other lifeless object and describe it as Christian. As far as I am aware, there is no Christian automobile industry, no Christian mathematics industry, and no Christian airline industry. Most people would probably find it odd if someone tried to start such an industry.

---

2   Gnosticism taught a salvation of the soul from the material world through gnosis, or a certain type of intuitive knowledge. The soul or spirit was good, the material world evil. The early church called it heresy.

Would painting a big red Jesus on the hood of a car make it a Christian car? Would a pizza with dove-shaped pepperonis or cross-shaped sausages be a Christian pizza?

A third reason I'm uncomfortable telling the stranger on the plane that I play Christian music is because it begs the question: What exactly is Christian music?

Is it a musical style? No. Saying that I play "Christian music" says nothing about the actual music. It could mean that I direct a large church choir, sing tenor in a southern gospel quartet, or play electric guitar in a Christian hardcore metal band.

Is it music made by Christians? No. There are plenty of Christians who aren't categorized in the Christian genre. There are also people in the Christian music industry who are not Christians. Our road manager, Heath, recently had a conversation with an artist who is pretty well known in many parts of the world for writing Christian music. Heath was asking her about her life, and asked where she we went to church. She laughed and told him that she wasn't into all of that stuff. She told him that she is not actually a Christian. She just knows how to write the stuff that Christians like to hear.

Most people probably assume that Christian music is categorized as such because of the content of the lyrics. This would be odd, because no other music is categorized by the content of its lyrics. There is no Buddhist or Atheist section of a record store. There is not a "gay" section or a "money" section. The only exception is Christian music,[3] but if Christian music is categorized by the lyrical content, what does it mean for a lyric to be Christian? Singing about Jesus? But there are plenty of mainstream acts that sing about Jesus, and plenty of "Christian" songs that don't mention Jesus at all.

---

3   Some might argue that "Latin" music also is categorized by lyrical content, but I would argue that this separation is about a language difference, not the philosophical content of the lyrics.

David Crowder Band* was a band that was marketed as Christian, but they sometimes covered songs from different mainstream artists like Sufjan Stevens, Hank Williams or Sinead O'Connor. They didn't change the words of the songs to make them "more Christian" or anything. They didn't put a sermon or a prayer in front of those songs. They just sang the songs. Which leads to odd developments—the Sufjan Stevens' song "O God, Where Are You Now?" was labeled as Alternative when Sufjan recorded it, but when David Crowder Band* recorded it, the same song became "Christian." What's even weirder is that Sufjan Stevens is a Christian.

If the determining factor of what falls into the Christian genre has nothing to do with the music, is not based on the content of the lyrics, and is not based on the personal beliefs of the artist, what could it possibly be? Is it simply that the music is released by labels that call themselves Christian?

Three major labels represent over eighty percent of the market's music: Universal, Sony, and Warner. These labels own most of the other significant labels in the world, including the Christian ones. Pretty much everybody in the music industry ultimately works for the same people. Whether you buy a Michael W. Smith album or a Marilyn Manson album, you are still paying the same small group of executives at the top of the food chain. So does being in Christian music simply mean that you are signed to one of the "Christian" marketing arms of the big three labels?

No, because there are also artists like myself who are not signed to a Christian label, but are labeled as Christian artists. Our band was signed to little indie mainstream label in Atlanta called Brash Music. Brash is not a Christian label. To my knowledge, they don't even have any Christians on staff. Yet, somehow our music is still always relegated to the Christian music industry.

So what is Christian music? I think I can finally answer the question. It's music made for Becky.

Becky
Like all genres, Christian music is simply a category that marketers use to reach a certain type of consumer. It is a marketing channel used to reach a very specific subculture.

This is further attested to by the common separation of "Christian" and "Gospel." While "Gospel" actually is a bit more consistent in its musical styles and sounds as a genre than "Christian" is, there is another primary difference between the two terms. For the most part, Christian music is made by white people and Gospel music is made by black people. You don't normally hear black people on "Christian" radio, and you don't normally hear white people on "Gospel" radio. These categories have more to do with subcultures than Christianity or the Gospel.

The subculture that buys Christian music couldn't accurately be called *the* Christian subculture. A Christian music executive at one of the big labels recently told me that the entire demographic that buys Christian music is only about two million people. Two billion people in the world consider themselves Christians. So only about 0.1% of people who consider themselves Christians buy Christian music.

0.1%

Christian music is not marketed to Christians so much as it is marketed to a very narrow subculture of a certain type of Christian. For years, Christian music marketers and radio programmers have known who their target demographic is. They actually have personified this target demographic, and her name is "Becky."

If you think I'm joking, ask any Christian radio programmer about her. A lot of stations have very specific information based on reams of market research. One station programmer told me that Becky is a forty-two-year-old soccer mom. She has three kids and she has been married twice. She is an evangelical Christian, but not a radical who watches Christian television or goes to church three times a week. She only attends church once or twice a month. They know what her favorite restaurant is. In fact, they know what restaurant she likes to eat at with her husband on a date and which restaurant she likes to take the kids to. They know the movies she watches and how she spends her money. She is the one who runs her household, the one with her finger on the radio knob, and she wants something positive to play in the minivan as she drives her kids to soccer practice.

Becky is the quintessential Christian radio listener.

Of course, this doesn't mean that everyone who listens to Christian radio fits this description. It simply is the bull's-eye of their demographic. If they aim at Becky, they get the most other people along with her. When Christian radio stations target Becky, they experience a vast increase in their numbers. They get specific in their targets for a reason. For years, they didn't target Becky, and they couldn't understand why they couldn't compete with the bigger mainstream stations. Now they can. This is how the entertainment industry works no matter what sort of categories they use. They target the demographic that will allow them to get the biggest numbers.

I once had a writing session with an artist who couldn't stop talking about Becky. He told me from the beginning that he really needed a song that would resonate with Becky. I asked if maybe we could just write something that felt honest and true to us. He said okay, but he really needed Becky to be okay with it as well.

Every idea I brought up was immediately brought through the Becky filter.

What about this?

Well, that's cool, but I'm not sure how Becky would feel about that.

Okay, what about this?

Listen, I personally like it. It's edgy and provocative and musical, but I really don't know what Becky would think about that.

I asked him what Becky would think if I shoved my guitar up his... well, not really—I'm not that clever when things get tense. Instead, I just start seething and retreating into my inner world. So that's what I did, and we eventually just gave up and left.

I don't actually have a problem with radio programmers talking about Becky. The stations know who their listeners are and program accordingly. It's smart.

I do have a problem with artists talking about Becky.

When the artist starts talking like the marketers, you know he has stopped listening to the Voice. The Voice doesn't speak in marketing terms, but in terms like truth, beauty, and passion.

The artist ought to listen to the voice inside, not Becky.

When the creator listens to the external voices, those voices will eventually lead her to sell out. They will lead her to put her art in the cookie cutter and cut away all of the dough that falls outside of the edges. But the edges are what make her who she is. The edges are good.

This is why there is so much soulless music in our society. Our artists are listening to the wrong voices. This seems to be especially true in the Christian music industry, which is another reason I feel uncomfortable telling the stranger on the plane that I play Christian music.

Zombie Music

Art that is laden with heavy messages can feel like soulless propaganda. Think of corporate jingles. Would you ever walk down the aisle at your wedding to a full-length version of a McDonald's corporate jingle? If you were to make a playlist for the birth of your first child, how many of the songs would you want to be advertising jingles? Not many? Why not? Jingles are catchy. But most people would never include them in such special occasions, because corporate jingles have no soul.

Folgers Coffee had a competition recently with a big cash prize for anyone who could write a new jingle for them. The song that ended up being chosen is actually pretty cool. It has all the elements of the laid-back indie singer-songwriter drinking a cup of coffee. Pretty melody, nice sultry vocals, warm acoustic instruments. But there's no soul to it. Because it's a freaking Folgers jingle. Who is going to put that on their iPod and just groove to it all day?

A song like that is what I call a musical zombie.

A zombie looks like a human. It eats like a human. It walks and makes noise and resembles a human. But it's a zombie. It has no soul.

Christian music is filled with zombies. The message of the music is predetermined, so we just need a form of music that can carry the message to a broad group of people.

"Well, let's see, hardcore music is pretty popular with the kids right now. Let's insert some Jesus language in that!"

Good music has soul, and the soul matters more than the form. You can't subtract the anger and angst from most hardcore music and still retain the essence of the music. Musical expression is not limited to just the notes and rhythms of a piece. Music is human. And if you take out the human bits and leave just the technical bits to be reproduced as carriers of whatever message you want it to carry, you no longer have a living thing. You have an un-dead thing. You have a musical zombie.

That's why a lot of Christian music feels contrived and lifeless. It's like a Folgers jingle because it has separated the message and the medium into two different things. This is also why much of the Christian industry is behind everybody else by five or ten years. Much of the Christian industry is like a beggar walking behind the rest of culture, picking up the crumbs of her marketing slogans and creativity to be used for our own purposes.

got milk?

That seemed to work well! Let's try it with our message!

got jesus?

This can make things difficult for artists who enjoy making music about God, but would prefer not to be associated with art that has been bastardized into propaganda for the religious right.

When people hear my thoughts about these things, they sometimes ask, "Well then, why are you part of the Christian music industry?"

My answer to that question is, "What do you mean?"

It's not like you sign up for a Christian music industry membership. I was signed to a mainstream label.

Most musical acts who are Christian have to intentionally distance themselves from the Church in order to have any success within the mainstream. As a result, there are loads of Christians in the music industry who wouldn't dream of performing in a church because of what it would do to their reputation.

This makes it difficult for a lot of bands that work (or would like to work) in the mainstream music industry but don't want to turn their backs on their roots. Many of us love the Church and even *enjoy* playing in churches sometimes. But this sometimes limits our ability to work with the people who inspire us or to find opportunity beyond the Christian music ghetto.

For our last album, "Ghosts Upon the Earth," I wanted to try to find a producer to work with that I could respect and trust musically. I started dreaming about my ideal producer, and I found some contact info for a guy who has produced a lot of music that I really like. I sent a demo to him with a proposal and a budget, and he responded and told me that he loved it. He said that he had been listening to all sorts of stuff recently and just couldn't find the inspiration to do any of it, but that when he heard my stuff, it just clicked for him. He said that he played it for his friends and they all felt the same. He said he was excited to do it.

The song I sent him was "When Death Dies," which is lyrically ambiguous enough that the listener may not assume that it's necessarily "Christian." But as the conversation progressed, I felt that I needed to confess to him that I am often associated with the Christian industry, because I know that this can be a taboo subject in the music industry at large. So I told him that this had been the genre that our music had been classified in before, but that I really wanted to make a record that would speak to an audience outside of the one we had already reached. I explained that I wasn't interested in trying to get him to operate within any of those confines. I just wanted to make some good art. I put this in a quick email that I thought would serve as a courtesy to avoid any awkwardness in the future.

Suddenly, he was not interested in working with me. Maybe it was coincidence; maybe it wasn't; but that was not the only time that kind of thing has happened.

On multiple occasions, I've had musicians turn down work because they weren't comfortable with the Christian music thing. For instance, we recently contacted an artist whose music I really enjoy. We asked her if she would be open to touring with us. At first, when she heard what we are offering with crowd size, number of dates, and so on, she was very interested. Then she saw the venue list, which included some churches. "Wait . . . so is this a Christian tour?" Her interest was gone.

Imagine if this was the gay music industry, and people were being turned down for work with simply because they were gay. People would be outraged. There would be protests and lawsuits and public outcry. But it's okay not to work with someone because he is associated with the Christian music industry.

If this is the price we have to pay to make music that is meaningful to us, that's fine. Honestly, it's really not that heavy of a price. People have been sawn in half for staying true to their beliefs; I can deal with a few unanswered emails.

Liturgical Music
All of that said, I do think that some Christian music has an element to it that sets it apart from other kinds of music. I do write within a tradition of music that exists for something more than entertainment or even artistic expression. In this stream, we write music that is intended to make God *happen* within a community of faith. It is music that is often (though not always) intended to be sung by others. It is prayer. It is a sort of sacrament that allows a community of people to brush up against the future God in present space and time. It is music that intends to become worship. This is a specific artistic function, and for that reason, I wouldn't have a problem with this kind of music being separated into its own category or genre.

Some have called this music "Praise" or "Worship" music. For reasons similar to my disdain for the term "Christian music", I have a problem with this language as well. It imprisons the idea of worship into a very small box. For the Christ follower, worship ought not to be limited to a genre or the singing portion of church services. Worship is a way of life. It is an offering of a person's self in whatever capacity and condition he finds himself in. For Brother Lawrence, washing dishes was his primary method of worship. All good work can become worship. Relationship can become worship. Singing can become worship. But none of these things ought to be named worship in and of themselves for the same reason that marriage shouldn't be named "love." Love *can* happen in a marriage, but love and marriage are not always the same thing.

For this reason, I prefer terms like "Liturgical Music" or "Church Music." Liturgical music is categorically different than other types of Christian music that are intended to be "alternatives" to mainstream music. If this were a marketing category, there could be different subcategories of actual musical genres like "Liturgical Rock", "Liturgical Pop", "Liturgical Classical"... etc. (Even though I don't like the idea of genres, I realize they may be a necessary evil in the marketplace).

In my perspective, liturgy is a very broad idea. It is not limited to robes, stained glass and incense. Liturgy is simply public worship. Every church is engaged in some type of liturgy. Some use readings and Eucharist; others use fog machines and strobe lights. The liturgical space is a broad and open space for experimentation. In my opinion, there are plenty of mainstream artists that write music that would be appropriate for certain kinds of liturgical space. This space is largely unexplored right now, and there is so much room for creative experimentation.

For instance, there is a need (and plenty of room) in this space for lament. For prophetic railing against the powers that be. There is room for songs, poetry, and artwork that explores doubt, hope, joy, struggle and storytelling. The idea of liturgy is a broad idea, and if it had a category of its own, perhaps it could invite a surge of creativity into that space. I think that would be good for the Church right now.

In my opinion, the non-liturgical music that is currently labeled as Christian should be placed in the genres that are more appropriate to the actual musical style. Rock, Pop, Country… etc. Just because a song sings "Jesus" rather than "baby" doesn't make it categorically different than its musical equivalent. Of course, there are a lot of Beckys out there that do want a positive or religiously infused alternative to the typical bawdy lyrical content of most popular music. She wants music that she can play for her family without worrying about offensive lyrical content. Also, there are a lot of these Christian bands that would not survive the transition to mainstream. Becky is their audience, and she doesn't necessarily want to (or know how to) navigate within the huge rivers of mainstream music to find music that she feels is safe for her kids to listen to. So perhaps another category of "Positive Alternative," "Family," or "Religious" music could be started. Whatever the language, it should not be included in the same category with liturgical music, and it should not be called "Christian". It is a categorically different thing. (And since when was Christianity a safe, positive alternative for the family anyway?)

Of course, iTunes, Amazon, and the three major labels haven't been calling me to ask my opinion on all of this. Most likely, we liturgical writers will just have to grit our teeth and deal with the inappropriate and potentially harmful label of "Christian music." But perhaps if a few more of us started making an effort to secede from the Christian music ghetto in little ways and find ways of cooperating on liturgical experimentation, something could eventually change.

So what do I tell the stranger on the plane? Well, it kind of depends on my mood. I might tell him "Liturgical Post-Rock" and smile at his confused facial expression, or I might just say, "Well, it's kind of hard to explain."

All of my idealistic problems with the language and categories aside, I actually do enjoy being part of the Christian music industry in a lot of ways. There are amazing people in my industry who take their art seriously and have inspired me greatly. People who believe that ordering creation is a sacred task and have acted accordingly. People I'm honored to work with.

Also, I really do love Christians. As weird as we can get, there is something really beautiful about the Church. And I am grateful for the time I've been able to spend singing and making music with people who love Jesus.

The reason I am so passionate about the subtleties of this idea of Christian music is that I think the idea of creating music for liturgical space and spiritual connection is so full of potential. At our best, we are able to see glimpses of what it could be, but I believe that we could be and do so much more. Like all human cultures, we have a lot of weeds to pull. A lot of underlying roots that need to be cultivated and soil that needs tending. In my opinion, that's work worth doing.

Appendix 3:

A Snapshot of American Christian Music

At the time of this writing, these were the top ten purchased Christian songs in the United States:

1. My Hope Is in You – Aaron Schust
2. Hold Me – Jamie Grace
3. Someone Worth Dying For – Mikeschair
4. I Can Only Imagine – MercyMe
5. Courageous – Casting Crowns
6. Cinderella – Stephen Curtis Chapman
7. How Great Thou Art – Carrie Underwood
8. Blessings – Laura Story
9. Lead Me to the Cross – Chris and Conrad
10. Remind Me Who I Am – Jason Gray

Here are the approximate tempos of these songs:

1. 75 (Aaron Schust)
2. 136 (Jamie Grace)
3. 90 (Mikeschair)
4. 80 (Mercy Me)
5. 82 (Casting Crowns)
6. 156, in 6/8 time signature (Stephen Curtis Chapman)
7. 91 (Carrie Underwood)
8. 58 (Laura Story)
9. 79 (Chris and Conrad)
10. 93 (Jason Gray)

As you can see, these tempos are not nearly as consistent as pop music. But they are consistently a lot slower. The average tempo is 87.1BPM. The only fast tempo song on the list is Jamie Grace's "Hold Me." The Steven Curtis Chapman song appears by the tempo number to be fast, but since it is in 6/8 time signature, the pulse actually feels more like a slow song. Here is a graph of the tempos:

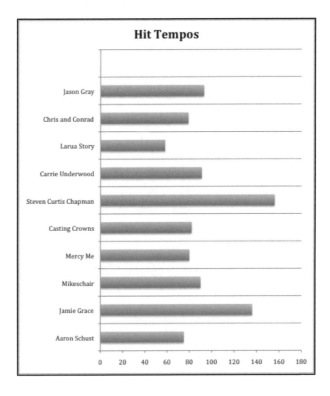

Chord-wise, the top three songs follow the same tendency with pop music, complete with repeating four-chord patterns. Whereas pop music has a more equal balance of minor chords and major chords, Christian music tends towards having far more major chords. All of these songs are in a major key. Also, the primary building blocks of the top Christian songs are 1, 4, 5, and 6 chords. In fact, there are only three songs in this list that use any other chords in their choruses. There are no non-diatonic chords in this list (that is, chords built on anything but the primary major scale).

At the top of the list, the patterns of the chords tend to more closely resemble pop music, just with more major chords. Also, like pop music, the top songs tend towards using the same pattern throughout the whole song. The farther down the list you go, the less formulaic the pattern of the chords becomes, though they generally still utilize one of the four primary chords (1, 4, 5, or 6).

Here are the primary chord patterns for the choruses of the songs:

1. My Hope is in You – 4, 1, 5, 6 (major, major, major, minor)
2. Hold Me – 1, 5, 6, 4 (major, major, minor, major)
3. Someone Worth Dying For – 1, 6, 4, 1 6, 4, 5 (major, minor, major, major, minor, major, major)
4. I Can Only Imagine – 4, 5, 1, 1/3 (major, major, major, major)
5. Courageous – 4, 1, 5, 4, 6, 1, 4, 1, 6, 5, 4, 1, 6, 5, 4, 1, 5 (major, major, major, major, minor, major, major, major, minor, major, major, major, minor, major, major, major, major)
6. Cinderella – 1, 2, 1/3, 4, 6, 5, 4, 6, 5, 1, 4, 5, 4/6, 5/7 (major, minor, major, major, minor, major, major, minor, major, major, major, major, major)
7. How Great Thou Art – 1, 4, 1, 5, 1 (major, major, major, major)
8. Blessings – 1, 5, 6, 1/3, 4, 2, 1/3, 4, 5 (major, major, minor, major, major, minor, minor, major, major)
9. Lead Me to the Cross – 4, 1, 5, 4, 1, 5, 4, 1, 5, 2, 1/3, 4, 5 (major, major, major, major, major, major, major, major, minor, major, major, major)
10. Remind Me Who I Am – 4, 1, 5, 6, 4, 1, 6, 5 . . . repeat . . . 4, 1, 5 (major, major, major, minor, major, major, minor, major, major, major, major)

It is my guess that what we will see in Christian music over the next several years is a move toward what the pop market is doing now. We will find more synths and less acoustic guitars. We may start hearing a few more minor chords. The tempos might get a little faster (unless the slower nature of the tempos is because there is a similar emotional temperature that the future Becky will be looking for). Just a guess.

Acknowledgments

I knew writing a book would be a lot of work, but *man*. It's a lot of work. I'd like to thank my wife, Lisa, for her support in this process. Aside from the countless conversations and ideas that she contributed to the content of this book, she made a lot of sacrifices giving me the time and space that I needed to write it. The longer I know this girl, the more I realize how lucky I am to collaborate with her, yet alone to be married to her.

I would also like to thank Bloom, my community of faith in Denver. Specifically, I'd like to thank Andrew Arndt, the lead pastor and one of my very best friends. He is one of the most underrated teachers in the world. He is brilliant, and his teachings and conversations have significantly contributed to the thoughts in this book. I'd also like to acknowledge our dear friends and fellow "fat kids" Jamie and Bre—thanks for all the late night conversations over "Say-Jay's" and "fro-yo" about these ideas.

Thanks to my band and co-conspirators over the years who have helped me grow and develop as an artist. Daniel Grothe, Michael Rossback, Cara Fox, Josh Harvey, Terence Clark, David Gungor, Rob Gungor, John Arndt, Josiah Bashta, and the many others who I have played music with. Thanks to Israel Houghton, JR Montes, Brian Smith, Calvin Nowell, and the folks at EMI publishing and Brash Music for their help in building this musical collective into a career.

Thanks to my parents and family who have always been so supportive of me and my artistic endeavors. Thanks for giving me beautiful stories to live and create from.

To my editor, Patton Dodd, I owe a great many props and thanks. I didn't know how important a good editor is until writing this book. Patton is brilliant and before his help, this book was a total mess.

And lastly, thanks to you, my readers and fans. I still am blown away that I get to do what I do for a living. Because of you, I get to spend most of the hours of my day doing the things that I love doing. Creating. I don't take that for granted. I love singing with you. I love dialoguing with you. Thanks for sticking with me as I experiment and explore. I'm honored to be on this journey with you.